A Salon at Larkmead

A Salon at Larkmead

a charmed life in the napa valley

Drew Sparks & Sally Kellman

 Ten Speed Press
Berkeley/Toronto

First published in 1999 by the Mills College Center for the Book, Oakland, California

A Kirsty Melville Book

Ten Speed Press
PO Box 7123
Berkeley, California 94707
www.tenspeed.com

Distributed in Australia by Simon and Schuster Australia, in Canada by Ten Speed Press Canada, in New Zealand by Southern Publishers Group, in South Africa by Real Books, in Southeast Asia by Berkeley Books, and in the United Kingdom and Europe by Airlift Books.

Cover Design by Jeff Puda
A Salon at Larkmead was designed by Peter Rutledge Koch at his Berkeley studio. The typefaces are Quadraat, a contemporary yet historically influenced Dutch text face designed by Fred Smeijrs, and Libra, an uncial script designed by S.H. De Roos for display.

Library of Congress Cataloging-in-Publication Data
Hitchcock, Martha.
A salon at Larkmead : a charmed life in the Napa Valley / [compiled by] Drew Sparks and Sally Kellman.
p. cm.
Largely diaries written by Martha Hitchcock from 1872 to 1897.
"A Kirsty Melville book"—T.p. verso.
Includes bibliographical references (pp. 138–41).
ISBN 1-58008-192-4 (paper)
1. Hitchcock, Martha—Diaries. 2. Women pioneers—California—Napa Valley—Diaries. 3. Pioneers—California—Napa Valley—Diaries. 4. Frontier and pioneer life—California—Napa Valley. 5. Country life—California—Napa Valley. 6. Elite (Social sciences)—California—Napa Valley. 7. Napa Valley (Calif.)—Social life and customs—19th century. 8. Napa Valley (Calif.)—Biography. 9. Coit, Lillie Hitchcock, b. 1843. I. Sparks, Drew, 1939- II. Kellman, Sally, 1948- III. Title.
F868.N2 H64 2000
979.4'19—dc21 99-058480

First printing, 2000
Printed in China

1 2 3 4 5 6 7 8 9 10 — 03 02 01 00

To our mothers

Contents

Acknowledgments

We extend our sincere gratitude to Janice Braun, Special Collections Curator, F.W. Olin Library, Mills College, and her staff; and to Peter Rutledge Koch for providing us with his design for this edition.

Special thanks to Caroline Herter, whose vision matched our own, and to Kirsty Melville and Holly Taines White for guiding our book to publication.

Thank you to The Bancroft Library and Bonnie Hardwick, especially for making available the cooking journal of Lillie Hitchcock Coit. The California Historical Society, the Society of California Pioneers, and the San Francisco History Center, San Francisco Public Library were also most generous in their support.

In the Napa Valley, our appreciation to J. Randolph Murphy, Curator, Napa Valley Museum and to Collections Curator, Betty Cumpston and the Sharpsteen Museum for their dedication to the preservation of regional history. Thanks also, to the St. Helena and Calistoga Public Libraries, whose newspaper archives proved invaluable.

Our gratitude to Marc H. Greenberg for his generosity and good counsel, to Ken Coupland, always in our court, and to Stefan Schinzinger, a partner in the project. Finally, a hearty thank you to all those who recognized our commitment and responded in kind, especially Joice Beatty, Blanche Brann, Meg Daley, Ella Ellis, Buzz and Betty Foote, Julie Glantz, Kathleen Kernberger, Mary Louise Kornell, Jennifer Lamb, Louise Lucas, Marjery Foote Meyer, Michael Olmert, Rolf Penn, Catherine Sparks, Catherine Stocker, Hannah Tandeta, Laurie Thompson, Maggie Weston, John York, and Peggy Ziegler.

Introduction

Napa Valley needs not the services of the poet. It sings its own praises and speaks for itself. Here, nature has been so lavish in her gifts, that man can add nothing to heighten the charms nor enhance the worth of this veritable Eden.

ST. HELENA STAR, 1888

California has long symbolized the fulfillment of the American dream, the pot of gold at the end of the westward migration, where hills bathed in sunlight meet the mysterious blue Pacific. In the popular imagination, California is golden, a land of sunshine and optimism, a place of bounty and pleasure.

If California invites thoughts of an earthly Paradise, perhaps the epicenter of Paradise can be found a short distance north of San Francisco in the Napa Valley. A cozy thirty miles long and only a few miles wide, it is a pleasant place blessed with woods and streams, wildlife, curative mineral springs, and perfect climate.

Martha Hitchcock and Lillie

The region attracted a discerning people who saw in the idyllic landscape a world of opportunity. Accordingly, they planted vineyards, established wineries, built resort spas, and so refashioned Napa Valley from wilderness to garden.

In the late nineteenth century, Larkmead, a sprawling bungalow surrounded by orchards, gardens, and vineyards, was the setting for dinner parties, charades, dancing and bouts of talk, star gazing, and poetry. Hosting this stylish bohemian salon was the legendary Lillie Hitchcock Coit.

Best remembered as San Francisco's "Firebelle," Lillie Hitchcock was an audacious child in a freewheeling gold rush town of few children. As mascot of the city's heroic early fire volunteers, Lillie defied the constraints of her conservative upbringing and embodied the spirit of frontier California. Her affiliation with the Knickerbocker 5 brigade became a lifelong pride and passion. When she was made an honorary member, she added "5" to her signature and monogram. The "Firebelle" sobriquet has carried Lillie's memory forward a century, and today the landmark tower named in her honor embellishes San Francisco's skyline.

Born in 1843 at West Point, New York, Lillie was the only child of Charles and Martha Hitchcock. Martha Hunter was raised on a North Carolina plantation, where she enjoyed the privileged traditions of the Antebellum South. In 1836, she married Charles Hitchcock, an Army surgeon, and regretfully left her family and sheltered life behind.

In 1851, the Hitchcocks were transferred to San Francisco, a booming seaport giddy with gold fever. They were welcomed into the Chivalry, a polite fraternity of transplaced Southerners that dominated the young city's social and political life. Situating themselves in apartments at the Occidental Hotel, the Hitchcocks cultivated an intellectual circle that included writers Ambrose Bierce and Bret Harte and humorist George Derby. These literary friends recognized the merit of Martha Hitchcock's own writing and encouraged her to publish. She considered it unseemly for a lady and confined her witty, often acerbic observations to her diaries.

On the eve of the Civil War, California voted to side with the Union, and Dr. Hitchcock sent his outspoken wife and daughter to live in Paris and wait out the war. Bright and stylish, Lillie translated Confederate documents for Napoleon III and captivated the French court with renditions of California mining songs.

In 1867, Martha and Lillie returned to a San Francisco turned upside down. The Transcontinental Railroad and the fabulous wealth of Comstock silver were bringing a new flood of opportunists and fortune seekers west. Fantastic mansions sprouted on Nob Hill, and former chambermaids sported diamonds at the Opera House. Martha Hitchcock regarded them as "Yankee vulgarians and Nothing People."

Lillie rejected a dozen eligible suitors, then to her mother's dismay, eloped with an enterprising Yankee, Howard Coit. The Hitchcocks bought their son-in-law a seat on the Stock Exchange, but quietly amended their will. As long as Lillie was Coit's wife, she would receive no inheritance. At a time of delirious speculation in Comstock silver, Coit became Chairman of the San Francisco Stock Exchange.

The marriage was a failure. On another floor of the same hotel where he shared a suite with Lillie, Coit installed his mistress. She was Mamie Emerson, wife of Billy Emerson, "The Big Sunflower," Irish tenor and leader of a popular blackface minstrel troupe. When Lillie discovered her husband's liaison, she demanded a divorce. Coit refused, claiming that Lillie was "the only woman I ever truly loved." Lillie ordered papers of separation, drank a solemn toast in champagne, and left San Francisco.

In 1873, the Hitchcocks had purchased a thousand acres in the upper Napa Valley, between the towns of St. Helena and Calistoga. Martha Hitchcock chose a homesite

Howard Coit   "The only woman I ever truly loved."

in the wooded western hills along the banks of Ritchie Creek and named it "Lonely." Not since her early life on a Southern plantation had she been so at home. She set about establishing trout ponds, vineyards, and orchards, and the rose hedges that would become her particular joy.

A short distance from Lonely, on the valley floor, the Hitchcocks set aside a few hundred acres for their daughter. Here, some seventy miles from the hum and bustle of San Francisco, Lillie built an Indian bungalow in the shape of a Maltese cross.

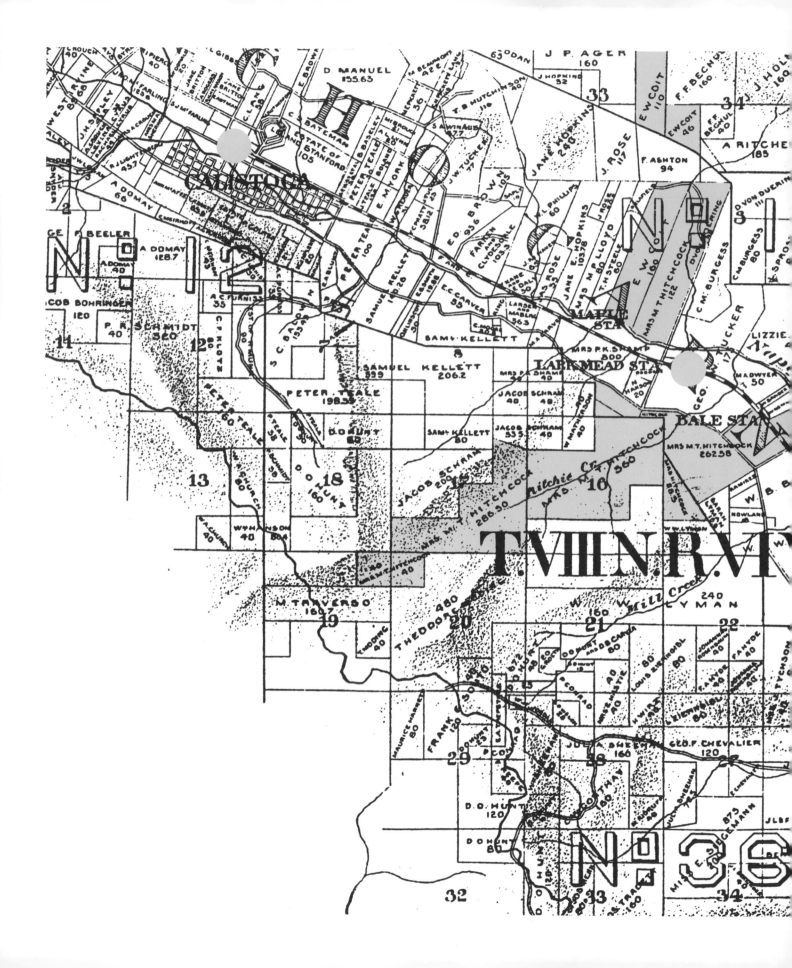

Intersecting corridors, twenty feet wide, invited cool evening breezes, and sweeping verandahs offered valley views in every direction. She employed Chinese servants, a French maid, and a local boy to be her hunter. Charmed by the songs of larks in the meadow, she named the place "Larkmead."

Lillie had always attracted a lively set, and Larkmead was well situated to entertain them. White Sulphur Springs, a fashionable resort spa in the hills above St. Helena, had introduced a smart clientele to the pleasures of Napa Valley. Just north, the town of Calistoga boasted millionaire Sam Brannan's spa and the tasty Chicken Soup hot spring. The spectacular Geyser Springs were a rollicking stagecoach ride beyond.

The Petrified Forest and the Palisades were among the region's geological wonders, and forests and streams offered opportunities for both sportsman and photographer. Here and there, a stately residence crowned the lush vineyards of a promising young wine industry. Neighbors Tiburcio Parrott, Charles Krug, the Beringers, and Joseph Schram opened their homes and wine cellars to Lillie and her guests.

Professors Joseph and John LeConte were fellow Southerners and frequent houseguests. They came west in 1869 to take part in the organization of the new University of California where they both served terms as President. John LeConte's analysis of the mineral waters at White Sulphur Springs revealed a sulphur content comparable to the great spas of Europe, an endorsement that further enhanced the resort's reputation.

His brother, Joseph, a natural scientist and a founding member of the Sierra Club, led a University expedition to Yosemite. Of his early years in California, Joseph wrote, "the climate, the splendid scenery, the active energetic people and the magnificent field for scientific and especially geological investigations stimulate my intellectual activity to the highest degree."

Young Porter Garnett was a favorite family cousin and a protégé of Lillie's. His parents urged him to end a prolonged summer holiday at Larkmead and return to San Francisco to attend business school. Porter went on to become an important member of the Bohemian Club, a creator of the avant garde periodical, *The Lark*, and later, a distinguished fine press printer. Eventually, he would build a home in Knight's Valley, constructed, in part, of timbers from the Larkmead bungalow.

Joaquin Miller, flamboyant "poet of the Sierras," was equal parts prolific writer and authentic bohemian. He often wrote at Larkmead and dedicated an occasional poem to Lillie. In great flowing beard and frontier garb, Miller had created a modest sensation in England. Back in California, he bought seventy-five acres in the Oakland hills, planted thousands of trees, built impromptu monuments to his literary heroes, and lived with his mother, Miss Alice, in a cathedral-like cottage. Miller's *Utopia*, published in 1880, imagined "a city on a high, watered and wooded slope . . . with only health, comfort and beauty to be considered." Late in the poet's colorful career, he wore his long gray hair braided into rat tails, the tips dyed a bright orange.

From San Francisco, the journey to Napa Valley was an event in itself, requiring two ferries and two trains and providing opportunities for chance meetings and exchanges of news and gossip. When visitors arrived by train at Bale or Larkmead Stations, it was an occasion. It was customary for them to stay a while.

The house parties lasted for days, a jumble of guests spilling easily from Larkmead's verandahs to Lonely's trout ponds. Picnics were plucked from the garden. A wildcat trapped in the attic dined on grapes and sugar. Evening tables lit by oriental lanterns were laden with delicacies and displays of roses, and always, plenty of wine. Throughout Napa Valley, it was generally agreed that, "Larkmead is the hottest place in the Valley and Lillie is the flame."

Martha Hitchcock

"Such a life of confusion and excitement," wrote Martha Hitchcock. Day after day, year after year, in a minute and deliberate hand, she entered her day's activities in small leather bound diaries, gifts from her daughter, Lillie. "California is the land of plenty. I know what it is to make an Eden out of a wilderness."

Martha pruned her roses, bottled her wines, jams, and jellies, yet her lasting works are her diaries. Here, she chronicles events both large and small. She itemizes her linens and her livestock, complains about the cook, delights in her garden, worries about tramps and trespassers and frets over a hand lost at poker. Yet, in spite of the vicissitudes of country life a century ago, the hard work, isolation, and uncertainties, there is a powerful allure. Larkmead seems charmed, a place where larks sing, where grows everything sweet and good, where fellowship prevails.

The quest for perfection, the tradition of ease and hospitality Martha, Lillie, and their neighbors shaped, endures. Napa Valley's resort spas and mineral springs continue to hold promise of rebirth and healing. An industry devoted to wine still promotes an atmosphere of refinement and celebration. Napa Valley has become an icon, a theme park of the American good life, a mecca visited by over five million people each year.

Today, along the scenic Silverado Trail, three graceful palm trees mark the site where the Larkmead bungalow once stood. The house is long vanished, its planks, timbers and artifacts added to other properties nearby. By the early 1890s, Lillie Hitchcock Coit had turned her attention back to San Francisco and ended her residence at Larkmead, which lay empty and abandoned for years.

The house at Lonely was destroyed by fire. The property is maintained as a popular state park. Still evident are traces of the foundations and paths, and the landscape so beloved by Martha Hitchcock.

Drew Sparks & Sally Kellman

Calistoga depot

Roses in Winter

A crowd gathered at the platform at the east corner of the depot where Alex Badlam had a fine large telescope in position, a camera and other necessary appliances for scientific observation of the total eclipse. The astronomers had erred slightly in their calculations for Calistoga, the actual line of totality being at Frank McDonald's place, five and a half miles west. Still, many agreed that the splendor of the eclipse was even greater than if total obscuration had taken place.

INDEPENDENT CALISTOGIAN, 1889

New Years Day. A great crowd of people went to Calistoga to watch the eclipse of the sun at 1 o'clock, that place being within the line of totality. Mrs. Noble, Col. Moseby and son, and Porter Garnett came by morning train. We got our smoked glass ready and watched it with much interest. It was so dark that great flocks of robins went to roost and the fowls sought their houses. The light was peculiar and the shadows, spectral. At the last moment, a luminous ring was visible around the black disc of the moon and a small point of the sun shone like a brilliant upon its circumference. Lillie said, "It looks like an immense diamond ring." After lunch, Col. Moseby and his son shot quantities of robins, while the rest drove to Schram's where they bought a half-dozen bottles of Schramsberg.

;ə

Chinese came to Lonely to see about making a stone fence. Offered them a dollar a yard and a horse and cart to haul the stone, which is most abundant. Afterwards, I walked down the creek bank to the bridge and across the hill above Tuckers' house, thence to the schoolhouse trail and back to the divide, surveying the route of the new road. Could see Lillie's house lying fair before me, only half a mile away.

;ə

Jim drove Lillie to St. Helena where she bought a half dozen chickens and six pounds of pork spareribs and tenderloin which we had for a simple breakfast with fricasseed fowls.

Chicken Fricassee

A chicken, cut in pieces	1 cup water
1 tablespoon flour	3 beaten egg yolks
1 tablespoon butter	The juice of a lime
1/2 teaspoon grated nutmeg	Mushrooms
Chopped parsley	Small onions
Salt & Pepper	Artichoke hearts

In your saucepan melt butter, add flour and stir. Add water, nutmeg, parsley, salt and pepper. Add chicken, cover, cook forty minutes. When cooking is two-thirds done, add mushrooms or if you like, small onions or hearts of artichoke. Thicken the sauce separately with the egg yolks and add the lime juice.

After breakfast we went to Larkmead. We went right to work planting the firs and maples on the north side of the lawn, the eucalyptus, elms and fig trees near the house, altogether twenty-eight trees in one afternoon. Showed gardener the grounds and how to lay off the walks and where to make the vegetable gardens.

જ઼

A frosty morning but a lovely day. Racked off two barrels of wine and put it in the upper cellar at Lonely in two barrels marked "Z." Philip cleaned the barrels with lime and soda and I sulphured them.

Pruned a good many rose bushes and made cuttings to give away. Trimmed the Solomon arches near the house and trained the Celine Forester rose vine which consumed time, then pruned the Cherokee rose hedge which was slow and difficult from the vast amount of growth. The young lemon tree is full of fruit.

Jim takes up roses for planting at Larkmead. Five Lamarques, twelve white Noisettes, three Rosamonds, three Baltimore Belles, two Cloth of Gold, all of which we carry to Larkmead and proceed to plant around the piazzas. Planted roses and passion vine near the dining room. Set out six rooted grapevines on the lattice by the kitchen and nineteen on the wall of the fowl yard. The ground is hard and rocky and it takes long to dig the holes.

Larkmead

Lillie is having a great deal of trouble with her well. The surface water is flowing in and it is thirty feet deep, so they cannot sink the last section of curbing, and the pump is not of sufficient capacity for keeping the water out. Rankin is rigging a derrick for lowering the curbing and for using the pump. He has four men pumping and is asking for four more men to pump night and day. He makes great pretensions about what he knows and what he can do, but I have no faith in him.

Before Lillie returned with men to help at the pumping, Rankin came to say that it was impossible to lower the water as it flowed in as fast as they could pump it out and that it was folly to try. So Rankin will close the well which Lillie concludes, for the present, to abandon.

&.

We drive to Bale Station and see our pigs in the neighbor's cornfield. Later, I learn that one of my pigs has been struck by the freight train, so badly hurt that Jim and Mase killed it, then sent for Philip to bring it up. Philip cut up the pig, very thin but sweet. A great pity to lose so fine a young sow. Being a thoroughbred Berkshire, she would have been very valuable. Saw the pork cut up and salted, as Philip has not much experience.

Made 22 pounds of sausage meat. Sent Jim a piece of pig, which Chinese like, a ham to Lillie, then worked the butter and afterward seasoned the head cheese. No time to rest, always so much to do. Don't wonder that lunatic asylums are full of farmer's wives.

The heaviest rain of the season fairly poured down upon us during Saturday and Sunday. Napa river was higher than at any other time, overflowing its banks and covering the greater part of Mr. Krug's vineyard with a sheet of water. White Sulphur Springs creek is said to have been higher by several feet than for some years past. So far, we hear of no bridges being washed away and conclude that damage done is slight.

ST. HELENA STAR, 1884

Rain, rain, nothing but rain. Three days ago, forty three inches had fallen in St. Helena to fifteen inches at this time last year. From the kitchen porch at Lonely, the creek is frightful. The roaring of the creek and thundering of the boulders as they go tumbling and crashing down the torrent keep us all awake and anxious. Andrew was up and down all night watching his hatching boxes, full with seven thousand trout eggs, afraid that the muddy water will destroy them. Never saw the water so high.

There was one break in the clouds which illuminated things, and that was a visit from my beloved friend, Dr. Joe LeConte. He seemed a visitor from another sphere, he is so far above the plane of ordinary mortals. He and his brother, Professor John LeConte to whom, by the way, I had just written a letter thanking him for the biography of himself taken from the *Popular Science Monthly*, an account of his scientific discoveries and works. I feel proud of the friendship of two such men. Joseph's only son is in the junior class of the University and is of an inventive turn of mind. He has built up a steam engine and connected it with all his machines in his amateur shop and laboratory. He is immensely clever and promises to make his mark.

Went with Lillie to Larkmead to help her plant trees. Andrew was on the far side of the creek with a wagon. We left ours on this side and crossed by Tucker's foot log. Lillie had a rope attached to the trees for me to steady by, and I crossed with fear and trembling. All the dogs were there. Clover, Ned, Guy, Bosilette, Fluffy and Chinchilla. Konick and Ring were left at Lonely. Only eight dogs!

Andrew dug two holes for trees and we planted them on the entrance side - a maple and an elm. I expected to plant half a dozen at least, but Andrew groaned and sweated, so Lillie decided to stop.

We drove to St. Helena, where I saw our neighbor, Mrs. Lyman. I bought two pounds of salmon for 35 cents from the St. Helena fish peddler. Lillie hired a Chinese man to dig holes for trees at Larkmead. The Express Agent gave to Andrew a letter and a little bag of silver, saying, "Take care of that package, it is a bag of money for Mrs. Hitchcock."

ॐ

About five o'clock this morning, Lillie and I were lying awake talking when we heard somebody at the dining room door. Thinking it was Jean, come after the letters for the morning train and that she was unusually early, I called her name but received no answer and the noise ceased. In a few minutes I heard a heavy body on the roof near our window. I rang the bell for ten minutes without awakening the servants. Lillie took my pistol and stood by the window ready to fire. I raised the bathroom window and shouted for Andrew and Jim. As soon as I called, the intruder ran down the ladder. When Andrew did come, there was nothing to be seen. We think that when the

Express Agent threw the package of silver to Andrew last night and called out "here is a bag of money for Mrs. Hitchcock!" that some tramp, stealing a ride under the cars, heard him and followed us up the canyon. The strangest thing is that the dogs did not bark - there were four here, and not one opened a mouth.

ɞ

I order the wagon for eleven o'clock but Mase Kinkel does not come and so I have to go with Otto to St. Helena. I wore my seal skin cloak and Jim wrapped up a stone bottle containing hot water and put it at my feet in the carriage. It was very cold and cloudy and before we reached St. Helena, it was snowing.

Went to the Carver's National Bank and got $125 for which I wrote a check. Went to the Post Office and the young woman helped me make out a money order, payable to D.T. Suddeth, Sheriff of Cherokee County, North Carolina.

Then I went to the Bank of St. Helena and Mr. Wade gave me my box of jewelry. I got him to bring it to the wagon and call it medicine, lest Otto might think it was gold and precious things and rob me. Then, I went to Bell's and ordered four sacks of barley for Lillie and bran, brown sugar, and candles.

After dinner, Lillie, Mase and I play poker and I had the worst luck. Once, I had a pat full and feeling sure of winning, bet rashly against a pat hand which Lillie held. When we showed our hands, she had four tens and took all the money.

I went to the Bank of St. Helena and Mr. Wade gave me my box of jewelry.

Ah Hing, the Lyman's Cook for 35 years.

Soon the Chinese Cook and a Fat French Maid

The house was a perfect Indian bungalow - wide porch all around and two intersecting halls twenty feet wide - the bathrooms being in the corners and the dining room and kitchen in an extension. With the doors of these intersecting halls open, it was possible to catch every breeze that blew, and the upper Napa Valley, near all those volcanic springs, can certainly be hot!

FLORIDE GREEN

They had quite an adventure at Larkmead with a buck which some dog ran into the vineyard near the barn. Lillie's greyhound, Chinchilla, caught it and threw it down twice and Ned, who was milking, ran and seized it by the horns and had a desperate struggle in which he was wounded. Lillie's hounds came up and diverted the attack, but it pursued Ned, who fled. Finally, his shouts brought help and Mase killed it, a three-pronged buck of which Lillie kept the head. I never before heard of a buck pursuing a man!

&

After luncheon, I went in one buggy with Morgan, and Philip drove Charlie to the large field to see the cows and calves. I counted Cherry and her four month old calf, Crumply, and her Jersey heifer, the yellow cow with her young calf, my Birdsall heifer with her calf, the two four year old steers, the bull, the yearling bull, Seekey. There is besides, a young Jersey bull of Major Simpson's on pasture, Dolly, Kittie, Miss Morgan, and the two colts belonging to Peterson's kin. Porter Garnett has written some rather clever verses about Morgan and Miss Morgan and has sent them by me to Lillie.

Porter Garnett has written some rather clever verses.

"An Equivocal Equine Excerpt"

A horse for his intelligence
Was famed in days of old
But I have a little anecdote
That knocks Black Auster cold

It was in Napa Valley
Where they crush the fragrant must
And where they never have a "boom"
Without they have a "bust"

A lane lay twixt two meadows
And 'neath a cloudless sky
The birds were winging merrily
While the gnats were also spry

A stallion seen approaching
Slowly upon the road
With a sun bonnet, a lady
And a buggy for a load

Old Morgan as they called him
Seemed to be deep in thought
Then a troup of horses spying
He greets them with a snort

The foremost is Miss Morgan
A filly full of nerve
Who meets her honored parent
With maidenly reserve

Now this fond and loving father
Seemed mad with very joy
And danced about the road-way
With other actions coy

And this tale is still related
By Old Morgan's mistress mild
How her sentimental stallion
Rejoiced to see his child

PORTER GARNETT

I look over the pickles and preserves and find 14 jars of sweet pickled peaches and nectarines, 2 of pickled cherries, 8 jars of preserved peaches, and 6 of mustard pickles. About half the preserved peaches are missing.

Sweet Pickle

10 pounds of peaches or plums	*3 pints of vinegar*
5 pounds of white sugar	*cinnamon and cloves whole*

Let the vinegar, sugar and spices come to a good boil, then put in the fruit and boil for 20 minutes. (The freestone peaches must be peeled previously). After the fruit has boiled 20 minutes, take it out carefully, and let the syrup boil down to a good consistency, then pour over the fruit in the jars. Cloves whole may be put in each plum or peach if desired.

Arrange glass jars and bottles and china. Find where my store room had been entered from the bed room which joins it, by the removal of three boards of the partition. When they were replaced, they were nailed with different nails and from the opposite or inside. From time to time, have missed a great many things, but could not understand it. Shall never know who was the culprit.

Busy all morning arranging household matters. Look over the bed linens, find 5 pairs linen sheets good, 8 pairs embroidered pillow slips, 10 pairs cotton sheets, 12 tablecloths, 5 dozen table napkins, besides cotton pillow slips and Marseilles quilts, two silk coverlets, one scarlet and blue, the other gray pearl and scarlet, a large Duvet covered with blue silk, and 12 pairs of blankets.

Duff Green drives up from St. Helena with his sister Floride and his mother, a very charming, chatty lady. She was a Miss Pickens of South Carolina and is very Southern in her speech and manner. She seems devoted to her son.

⁓

We drove by neighbor Schram's and I got out to look at the new house which is very nice, very large and convenient. I rejoice heartily in Mrs. Schram's prosperity. She has been so patient and helpful, so kind to everybody.

> *Among the numerous grape-growers in Napa County, very few have succeeded as well as Jacob Schram. He and Mrs. Schram have labored late and early, and with their close application in business, perseverance and good management, has come prosperity. They have erected a spacious dwelling-house, a mansion which cost several thousands of dollars, and will make a very pleasant home.*

Few have succeeded as well as Jacob Schram.

The basement is made of stone, constructed so that the second floor is level with the ground at the rear of the residence. There, one room is fitted up for an office for Mr. Schram, the other two, for bottling and storing wines. The main entrance is at the front, and a very wide verandah extends along the north side. The sitting room is spacious and pleasant with tinted, "sand finished" plaster walls and a ceiling of varnished wood. Behind it, a dining room, kitchen with range and sink, and beyond a pantry and laundry room.

The third floor has a linen room and three sleeping rooms to be occupied by Mr. and Mrs. Schram and their son, Herman. As regards ornamentation, Herman's is the finest room in *the house. The ceiling is nicely frescoed with two pieces of fine art-work, one of which is allegorical, done by a San Francisco painter who also superintended the tinting and other ornamental work.*

INDEPENDENT CALISTOGIAN, 1889

Lillie returned with a cook whose name is Ah Soon. When she crossed Napa Creek, Lord and Morgan and Charlie sunk to their bellies in quicksand. It was a narrow escape.

Jim went to Calistoga to get the horses shod. Northrup wants $3 for Morgan and Charlie, $6 for two pair of mules from Larkmead and 50 cents to mend the neck yoke.

Sent for cuttings of Muscat of Alexandria, Black Malvoisie, Zinfandel and Grey Reisling, the two latter considered the best grapes for wine. Will root them for Larkmead.

Philip took me to the upper vineyard where I wished to mark the grapes for cuttings. I didn't know the Burgundy from the Black Hamburg and shall be obliged to get Jim to mark them for me.

The Chinese Boss who runs the gang of stake cutters up the canyon surprised us by saying there were no more trees to cut. They had cut down ten trees, some eight feet in diameter, and had only 1,300 stakes made. They must have wasted the timber. Mase had assured us there was timber enough in one tree to make 2,000 stakes. He is either a liar or an idiot, perhaps both.

Chinese men

Jim dug up the two elm trees and took up the five magnolias and the four orange trees in boxes which I have been keeping for Lillie a year, and we packed them in the wagon and drove to Larkmead. Creek banks very boggy.

We find paperers at work nailing up wall cloth and Rankin scraping dining room walls. Lillie's range, the pipe and the sheet iron came on the freight train at noon. By steady work, Steves the plumber had put it up by 7 o'clock.

Capt. Sayward came early this morning to see Lillie about building the bridge. Says if he is elected roadmaster, will try to get the appropriation and wants Lillie's influence with Burgess and the Tuckers.

Lillie got a letter from Allen Knight that he and his wife will come Saturday. Also a letter from Dr. and Mrs. Whitney, who will be up after they visit the quicksilver mine above Calistoga, in which they are interested.

Lillie's bathtub arrives. Steves comes from St. Helena to finish the pipes for the range. Makes a new chimney and puts the governor on the tank in order. Finally it is fixed. He undertakes to do something to the bathtub vent but does not succeed very well. Rankin cuts a trap door in the ceiling of the butler's pantry and Buster puts away carpets, trunks and odds and ends. Lillie has a letter from Townsend with some patterns of tiles, and a bill from Hammond the tinner for fixing the bathroom.

❧

Mr. and Mrs. Knight arrive by morning train. They drive with Mase to Calistoga to meet and fetch Dr. and Mrs. Whitney. It made dinner late, but it was very pleasant.

Lillie, Mr. and Mrs. Allen Knight, Maggie Randolph and Duff Green drove over from Larkmead to make me a visit. They were very jolly and promised to come tomorrow to make photographic views of the place.

❧

Charming, like a May morning. Daphnes and violets fill the air with fragrance. The almond trees have been in bloom for a fortnight, the peaches and apricots are just like rose banks and the camellias are in their glory. The yellow jasmine has finished along the hillsides, but the cyclamen are thick and pretty, the blue flowers of the borage, the anemones and Indian plumes are all here after their long absence, and all the woods are gay in February. Was there ever such a climate.

Lillie and all her guests drove over to make photographic sketches of Lonely. Found Lillie dressing in my grandmother's blue and silver brocade court dress to be photographed by Mr. Knight. Lillie's maid, Eugenie, said she looked like an angel.

Lonely

"She looked like an angel."

Such a dismal day. Sun never shone at all. As if to increase the gloom there was an awful row in the kitchen. Joe and Soon disputed about sawing some wood and Joe struck Soon on the forehead with a cup of wine and they fought. I heard the noise and ran into the kitchen where I saw Joe holding Soon by the queue with one hand and pounding him with the other while Soon held Joe around the legs and little Jim was struggling in the hands of Eugenie and fighting Joe with all his might. I tried to stop the fight but had no effect. I seized one of Soon's wrists and one of Joe's and tried to loose them but could not.

I was afraid Joe would draw his knife or that little Jim would pick up one of the carving knives lying on the table and inflict a dangerous wound. Finally, Soon threw Joe to the floor and I cried "help." In a moment everybody was out of bed. Mrs. Whitney ran out barefooted on the damp verandah. Mrs. Knight rushed to the kitchen window but could not get in and Dr. Whitney shouted to them to stop. By this time the parties were breathless and exhausted and were separated, but everyone was excited and anxious all day.

Joe said he wanted to leave and I told him that Mrs. Coit would pay him and send him by afternoon train and he went off swearing and white with rage. Eugenie behaved like a perfect idiot, crying and swearing by turns, exclaiming that Lillie and I liked Chinamen better than white men and that she should quit at the end of the month.

Mase drove Joe to the station and he went to St. Helena very reluctantly, told Mrs. Coit that he never expected to leave her and did not wish to go, but all in vain as his conduct in attacking the cook was inexcusable.

Philip woke Mase to tell him that Chinchilla had been found dead with a bullet hole thro' him, on the railroad track this morning. We rushed to the station and asked Mr. Connor, who said there was no bullet hole, that the dog had been struck by the cow catcher and killed instantly. The railroad men had covered Chinchilla with earth, but they uncovered him, and Mr. Connor took him in his arms and brought him to the buggy. Mase will bury him tonight. Felt much saddened, as Chinchilla was the most beautiful dog I ever saw and possessed of a wonderful intelligence. He had won a famous race at the Merced Club and was altogether a remarkable dog.

೫

Sayward comes while I am at dinner and talks about the Larkmead bridge. Supervisors have voted 400 dollars and he wants 200 more. Evidently he thinks Lillie will give that. I told him he was mistaken.

He and Miss Hastings will be married the 15th.

Miss Hastings' Engagement Visit

To show how well our matrimonial bureau is taking, we print the following, which is a bid for the hand of No. 1, mentioned in last week's Bachelor List: Dear Sir, Pardon me for addressing you thus, but this being leap year, all the young ladies have the same opportunities that are granted to young gentlemen. Upon inquiry, I learn you are a gentleman of good society, with cultured ways and considerable wealth. Also, that you are in the decline of life and in need of a companion to cheer and comfort you. I think a lady with long, auburn tresses flowing fancy free will about fill the bill. Hoping a favorable reply, I will anxiously await it.

ST. HELENA STAR, 1888

Malcom Garnett, Miss Friedlander, a tall handsome woman, and her niece, Bessie Bowie were with Lillie today, and I saw Bessie Bowie for the first time. It seems yesterday that I saw her mother at the old White Sulphur Springs. She was there in the prime of her life, young, pretty, stylish and admired, the idol of her parents who surrounded her with everything which the heart of a young girl could desire. Mr. Bowie was just growing interested in her and was dividing his attention between her and Cora Lyons, who was her guest. They used to ride on horseback over the hills and drive through the valley and wander up the canyon and picnic and gather flowers. That was twenty years ago, and now this grown up young woman comes in her mother's place to make a visit.

Miss Friedlander is very depressed about her niece's marriage. Thinks marriage is such a risk, and her niece so young. Nothing makes me sadder than to see a marriage, and I never go to a wedding if I can help it. A funeral is not half so sad, for there one's troubles are ended, while in a marriage, they have just begun.

Malcom Garnett and Lillie had a fierce discussion about pretty women and sensible women. Lillie insisted that men preferred pretty looks to plain, clever women. Mallie took the opposite side, and I tried to pacify them by telling them that rich women were preferred to either.

Jerome has returned from China, and he and Miss Hastings will be married the 15th and sail immediately for China. They will come to Larkmead Thursday to make Lillie a short visit. Mrs. Hagar sent me recipes for pickled figs and cantaloupe.

⁂

Got everything in readiness for my expected guests who arrive before twelve. Miss

Hastings, Mrs. LeBreton, Maggie Randolph and Lillie. They fished in the creek and caught several trout. Buster made beautiful decorations of flowers and ferns and the whole place looked lovely. Had a nice luncheon, fruits and coffee on the verandah. We drove then to Larkmead by way of Mrs. Schram's and Mrs. Shamp's. At the former, we took a glass of Golden Chasselas and at the latter, some fine cherries. Seven o'clock dinner at Larkmead and music afterwards by Mrs. LeBreton who plays the piano charmingly. Then a little dancing. They all sing and dance "Carfoogleman, Daughter of the Barber," which I heard Carrie Simms sing in Paris.

৯

I received some okra seeds of a new variety which I gave to Jim to plant. Already the young plants of his first sowing are beginning to appear, giving promise of succulent pods and future gumbos. Somehow we never have too much okra. If the whole garden was full of it, we should eat it all. Every day in the summer, we have okra gumbo and we never tire of it. If any is left from gumbos and stews, we dry it and make soup of it in the winter. So Jim has orders for an abundance of okra.

৯

May Day. Canyon full of picnic parties, hundreds of people. The Presbyterian and Methodist Sunday schools picnic on our creek and they walk up here. A whole crowd of people, principally women and children, pour into the yard and explore the fish ponds and roam at will over the lawn. A Miss Beasley insists on coming in and proceeds to canvas for the sale of the Revised Testament. I am obliged to subscribe to get rid of her. Tom locks the gate and finally, we have peace.

May Day. Canyon full of picnic parties.

The Cherokee hedge is a white wall of beauty and the Lamarques are climbing up the eucalyptus trees and sending down long garlands which shake their fragrant blossoms in the wind. The onions are up and the potatoes several inches high. Peas are just making their appearance. Ambrose waters the strawberry vines, also the young lettuce, and we pick spinach to send to Larkmead where fifteen men are planting grape cuttings. The grass and wildflowers are growing faster than the plough can destroy.

❧

Arose early on account of Mrs. Tucker's funeral which is to take place at ll. Gathered all the white roses I could for a cross which Buster made. Buster and I went to the funeral and there was a great crowd. She was only forty-three and left a large family of children and grandchildren. The Shamps, Schrams, Lymans and all the neighborhood were there. Buried her at the little white church.

❧

Larkmead looked golden in the level rays of the sun and fragrant with myriads of wild flowers. Had a very nice dinner. I carried over champagne and we drank to the new house and those who dwelt therein. After dinner, we sat on the verandah while the piano was being brought in and Lillie played a little for me. I stayed the night and slept with Lillie, all the doors and windows open.

Lillie was not up but she called a goodbye to me. The larks were singing joyously in the grain fields and were so gentle that they scarcely flew away before the carriage wheels. Turtle doves were cooing in the trees, woodpeckers were hammering the

The Cherokee hedge is a white wall of beauty.

decaying trunks of the venerable oaks, and newly mated quails ran hastily into the brush from the gravelly roads where they had been strutting.

At Lonely, I found Jim with a bright smile and Polly fluttered and screamed and scolded with great fuss and feathers of delight to welcome me. Jim told me that he knew I had come, that Polly had told him so. She called "Mama, mama." He said, "You no come, she no talk. You come, she always talk."

so.

Decoration Day. Joaquin Miller arrived after having spent the day at the Veteran's Home in Yountville where he spoke at the decorations of the soldiers' graves. He is charming, so gentle, and sweet as a woman. Repeated a little poem of three verses he had composed on the turtle dove and gave to Joe Redding to be set to music. Has dedicated them to Lillie.

On the train, he saw Judge and Mrs. Lake and two daughters, one of whom has written a novel, *On the Verge*. Joaquin is going on a tour by the Northern Pacific to the Yellowstone and back by Denver to write up the scenery for *The Independent*. He is to receive $25 a day. Speaking of his success he said, "it has brought me so much money that I have got some new clothes and have bought mother a silk dress." Says he will spend some time at Larkmead when he returns.

Joaquin told me to read in tomorrow's *Examiner* the poem he has written on Cleveland. They are to pay him $50. He wrote it in a few hours, but it was hard to connect any sentiment with a cold, prosaic, matter of fact man with a bald head and overgrown stomach. He remembered seeing a letter Cleveland wrote to his brother when Cleveland became Governor of New York. In it he says, "Oh, if Mother could only have lived to see it." The poet seized on that incident for his text. He told me much of his idea for a future state. He believes that whatever we earnestly desire to be in this world, we shall become in the next.

We lunched on quantities of strawberries from the garden.

A Midsummernight Astronomy Lecture

One of her most welcome guests was Professor Joseph LeConte, an old family friend. He was that year, studying the Petrified Forest, which is not far from Larkmead. One hot starlit night everyone took a pillow to the verandah and stretched out on one of the twenty-foot steps, while Professor LeConte talked only as he could, with the simplicity of great learning, of the stars.

FLORIDE GREEN

Read in the papers this morning of the advent of a great comet which has suddenly made its appearance. Philip makes his appearance and tells me he has bad news for me. I am so frightened that I can scarcely stand. He tells me that two boys are discovered by him fishing in the large pond in the yard, and he seizes one boy and takes more than a dozen of my largest and finest trout. As the fish are alive, hoping to save them, he throws them back in the water and the boy escapes. He takes his rifle and dog and follows down the canyon but finds no one. I am thankful that matters are no worse and no one hurt, although I am sorry for the unfortunate trout.

Spent the day as usual at work. I have no leisure for enjoyment, there is always so much for me to do. Plums and apples are very abundant now, blackberries and a few figs. Planted beans for late crop and prepare ground for beets, turnips, parsnips and salsify.

In the wine cellar, bottled our old Port of vintage 1877. It is excellent. Ninety seven bottles and three demijohns. Tom planted rows of string beans in the garden and covered another cherry tree with rose colored mosquito net. Busy mending nets for the cherry trees. The mice ate them in holes last winter.

Lillie, Mrs. Hooker and Maggie Randolph, on their way to St. Helena, drove up to get some blankets and the bottle corker. Lillie expects Ned Hall and others Saturday night, to go fishing Sunday over St. Helena Mountain. I will have to make up beds for them. Her house is already full. Such a life of confusion and excitement.

❧

Early this morning, Lillie came over with Ned Hall and Mr. Hooker to fish our creek. Someone had been ahead of them. However, they got eighteen and returned before noon. The rest of the party, Mrs. Hooker and Joe Jones, came later, and we lunched on quantities of strawberries from the garden with pure sweet cream, fresh pound cake, trout and fried spring chickens.

Pound Cake

1 lb Flour   12 Eggs

1 lb Sugar   1 small wineglass of Brandy

1 lb Butter

Cream the Butter and Sugar together. Beat the eggs separately until light, add Flour to Butter and Sugar and then add small wine glass of Brandy.

Went into the orchard and gathered cherries. Quantities ripe under the nettings, but the birds are devouring the fruit on the uncovered trees. Linnets and thrushes and quails flew over and around me, as if they felt inclined to dispute possession.

I ordered the buggy and drove to Larkmead. The Burgess children were near the gate and seeing me coming, waited to open it for me. They had killed an immense snake, fully five feet long, and had stretched it across the road!

ॐ

Dr. Joseph LeConte came quite unexpectedly by the noon train, very glad to see him. Mase went to the three o'clock train and met Dr. John and Mrs. LeConte and Miss Bloodgood on their return from the Geysers. They were sunburnt and tired to death. Mrs. LeConte was ill all night at the Geysers with a nervous attack.

Mrs. LeConte and Miss Bloodgood arose early, and the latter insisted on promenading the piazza in the gale which was blowing. She was arrayed in one of Lillie's

I went into the garden and gathered cherries.

kimonos, her traveling dress being very warm. Mrs. LeConte was dressed in her usual eccentric style, with her Mary Stuart head dress which she always wears. She has finished *On the Verge* and thinks it a remarkable production for a young girl. She is now reading Fanny Kendle's recollections, having known the Butler family.

John LeConte is as charming as ever, so patient and so fond of his wife. Would there were more like him! I have a talk with him on the future state and his visions. We discussed the sect of Second Adventists living here in this valley, their habits and doctrines. He thinks the world is getting tired of dogmas.

Anniversary of the LeContes' wedding. Forty years married and they are like two lovers. Buster goes for the Chinese lanterns to illuminate the grounds at Larkmead and makes a large marriage bell of ferns and roses which he hides until evening. He suspends the bell over the entrance to the verandah. Lillie detains the LeContes until everything is lighted up, and when she asks them to walk out, they are very much affected by the decorations. Soon cooked everything nicely and waited on the table. Everything went well until Mrs. LeConte found a small garter snake in the bathroom and the fright threw her into hysterics.

We go after dinner to the orchard to see the comet. It is very bright and looks like the peacock of stars, its tail pointed directly to the North Star.

❧

Arose rather earlier than usual. Lillie came driving her four-in-hand team with the filly in the lead and looked gay and happy. Mase driving us behind Miss Morgan and

Mrs. LeConte was dressed in her usual eccentric style.

White Sulphur Springs

Jennie, we drove to Calistoga but the gate being locked, could not drive into the spring grounds to taste the Chicken Soup spring. Thence to Tubbs', up and waiting breakfast for us.

After an hour's rest, we drove to Schram's where we visited the cellars and tasted his wines. Professor LeConte tried some which had been treated by electricity and thought it an improvement. Thence, to Beringer's where we walked thro' his subterranean cellar which was quite wonderful. We tasted his wines, white and red and the muscatels and ordered fine claret at 65 cents a gallon. Thence to St. Helena where I ordered strawberries and bought a yard of flannel.

On to White Sulphur Springs, where I was haunted by a hundred ghosts of yore. Tasted the water of the different springs, peered into the ballroom and the cottages and I got an awful fit of the blues. My poor old husband! How fond he was of this place and often he came here. But for this fondness, we should never have had this property in Napa Valley.

The Fourth of July

Ain't We Jolly?

The Fourth of July is drawing near, and the small boy is preparing to make his wonted amount of noise and smoke. Already, firecrackers, bombs and other villainous combinations are exposed for sale in St. Helena's stores. The Native Sons are quite active in making preparations for their celebration and have secured Mr. Cruey's grove for the barbecue. The picnic will eclipse anything of the kind ever had in Napa County. Preparations on an elaborate scale are being made, and everything is being placed in first class condition. A force of men is already busy clearing away the underbrush and leveling off the grounds, preparatory to erecting a large platform for dancing and for placing the different refreshment stands in position. The platform is to be 50 by 60 feet in size and a fine spot has been selected for it, which will be shaded for the entire day so that dancing will be comfortable, no matter how warm the weather.

That genial and patriotic gentleman Mr. Hanna was found busy supervising operations for the great barbecue. He had six men busily engaged, digging a trench 76 feet long, 4 feet wide, and 4 feet deep wherein the beeves are to be roasted for the occasion. Another trench, 10 feet long, 2 1/2 feet deep and 2 feet wide, is being dug for the cooking of the sheep. 8 cords of wood will be required to do the cooking. 6 beeves, 6 sheep and 6 hogs will be roasted, in the neighborhood of 3,500 pounds of meat, capable of feeding 3,000 people. Bushels of other delicacies will be served.

Captain Niebaum has given a hundred gallons of wine, 50 of red and 50 of white. John Hanna and L. Tully, assisted by Uncle Abe, a colored man from Napa, will have charge of cooking the steers. A bull's head lunch will also be served. Mr. Hanna says, if they are lucky enough to get a couple of fine deer, they will be placed on the bill of fare along with several fine spring chickens which he will only serve to his most intimate friends. Remember, the barbecue and picnic are free to all, and a general invitation is extended. Again we say Hurrah for the Fourth of July.

&

The Fourth of July. Slumbering St. Helenians were awakened early in the morning by the resounding echoes of exploding bombs and fire crackers in the hands of young America. The morning sun cast its rays on a town bedecked with a profusion of bunting, lanterns and from many housetops, the glorious stars and stripes of which every true American is proud. Patriotic citizens, each one seeming to be desirous of excelling his neighbor, displayed much taste in their arrangements.

At 10:15 the Procession was formed. First came the Grand Marshal, the Native Sons of the Golden West, then the Americus Fire Company No. 2 hauling their handsome hose cart, preceded by a brass band. Next, a carriage with the President of the Day, the Reader of the Declaration of Independence, and the carriages of the Pioneers and Town Trustees.

Following them were the Horribles. This grand parade of mighty and grotesque Squeedunks preceded by a costumed brass band from Yackahoula, was a motley crowd, even the beasts of the jungle being represented. They had with them their Orator, loaded brimful of "jib-jabs" for St. Helena townsmen.

The display wagons followed, gaily festooned with flags and bunting and making quite an array of advertising, George A. Riggin's Wonderful Wagon, The Wine Palace by Capt. Niebaum of Inglenook Cellar and J. H. Steves, being among them. MacKinder & Trainor had a nicely decorated outfit. Their motto was "We sell the earth, but in small lots."

That enterprising gentleman, Mr. Riggins, received his Wonderful Wagon last Tuesday from Stockton, a handsome rig that attracts much attention. It is designed for a traveling drug store and is most complete in arrangements and elaborate in detail. The iron work of the harness is heavily nickled and profusely decorated with silver bells and patent leather. The wagon is open through the center like a bus, has seventy-nine drawers, a canopy top, and a dozen little silver bells to make music wherever it goes.

Carriages of citizens brought up the rear as the Procession made its way to the picnic grounds at Cruey's Grove, where the day's program was carried out. The oration was a masterful effort. The speaker thought that indiscriminate immigration should be stopped, that our country should not be the place of refuge for the off-scourings of all nations. "We welcome a bold healthy white people, but we do not want the insane, paupers, nor the criminal classes who plant in our midst the vices of other countries."

At the conclusion of the exercises, it was announced that the barbecued meat and baked beans were

The Native Sons of the Golden West

in readiness and a general rush was made on all sides for those who were serving out the meat. Long tables had been built underneath the trees, with plentiful supplies of tin plates, spoons, salt and pepper thereon. Soon, groups of friends and acquaintances formed at the tables and under the trees and the huge sides of beef, mutton and pork began to disappear. The great cauldron of baked beans grew empty and the boxes of bread showed up missing. Misters Dowdell and Foss did some rapid carving and looked fine in their aprons and plug hats.

Dancing commenced on the platform and was kept up at a lively rate. About 2 o'clock a game of baseball began, the Wonderfuls of St. Helena defeating Calistoga nine to two in seven innings. Refreshment wagons and stands for the sale of ice cream, candies, lemonade and soda water, beer and wine did a fine business throughout the day. The Wine Palace was a particularly handsome affair and created quite a sensation. Captain Niebaum had taken his wagon into the grounds where he treated a number of his friends in "a very hospitable manner." Fully 3,000 people were in attendance at the grounds, a large number of them strangers loud in their praise of St. Helena.

In the evening, beautiful fireworks were sent up from many of our town residences, and those who did not burn money in this way had just as good a time sitting on their porches and watching the displays made by their neighbors.

ST. HELENA STAR, 1884, 1888
INDEPENDENT CALISTOGIAN, 1888

Refreshment wagons did a fine business throughout the day.

Joaquin Miller

God's White Tomatoes

Joaquin Miller, while writing the "Psalm of Syria," spent many weeks at Larkmead. He wrote in the morning and at night. Often, while the poet slept, Mrs. Coit and her guests would struggle to make ready his manuscript for the printer. One night, an undecipherable word stumped everybody. Mrs. Coit declaring it was "God's white tomatoes," decided to wake the author, who at first was as puzzled as the others. However, after reading the passage and getting the rhythm, he called out that it was "God's white tomorrows."

FLORIDE GREEN

Soon, the cook was in an awful humor because there was no one ready for breakfast before three o'clock. Floride slept until three and Lillie kept her bed until four. I told her she was a night-blooming crocus. The breakfast waited and Soon raged. He told me to tell Mrs. Coit to get another cook, that he would not stay longer. When I went to Lillie's room at four, I told her and she would have gone immediately to St.

Helena to look for another cook. However, she asked him when he would like to go and he said, "Sunday" and she said "All right." This is his gratitude for the kindness she has shown him.

Green Tomato Pickle

> *Select smooth green tomatoes. Slice 1/2 inch thick, salt overnight. Next morning, pour off the salt water. Put a layer of tomatoes in a kettle with a layer of onions sprinkled over with allspice, cloves, ginger, black pepper. Tablespoon full of brown sugar, with mustard and celery seed and parsley seed and a sprinkle of the best English mustard until the kettle is filled. Cover with vinegar and boil slowly until clear.*

Mabel Gray and I are busy with the wine half the day. We have sealed nearly all the Centennial white wine of the "Lillie" brand, which was made in 1876 and was our first vintage. We filled more than one hundred bottles, and still some remains. Mrs. Gray helped me a little and herself so much that she was tipsy before we were half finished. When the sun came out bright and pleasant, we walked up the canyon as far as the wood chopper's cabin. The woods were lovely. Also got a tick, which was not at all lovely.

Nothing but fruit. Peaches of every color and flavor and plums, red and yellow and purple and nectarines, red and white, and pears and apples until I am sick of the sight, besides the figs which hang neglected on the trees.

Arose early and went about the sweet pickles of damsons. Weighed 15 pounds of fruit and 9 pounds of white sugar and 3 pints of cider vinegar, 2 ounces of cloves and 2 of cinnamon. Put the sugar, vinegar and spices in the kettle and when the syrup boiled, put in the fruit and cooked it slowly until the syrup was clear. Then I put the plums in jars, boiled the syrup an hour and poured it over the fruit until the jars were full, and I sealed them.

I cut quantities of peaches for drying and made 10 pounds of sweet nectarine pickles, labeled my preserves and pickles and canned fruit, and put them away in the front cellar bin. There are 5 jars of peach marmalade, 6 jars of peach preserves, 7 jars of plum pickles sweet, 5 jars of nectarine pickles sweet, 6 jars of canned peaches, l jar of cherry preserves and 6 jars of nectarine pickles remain yet in the store room.

Peach Chutney

Peaches 12 lbs	Garlic 1/4 lb
Sugar 4 lbs	Mustard seed 1/2 lb
Raisins 2 lbs	Red Chiles 1/2 lb
Salt 1/2 lb	Green Ginger l lb
Vinegar 4 quarts	

Slice the peaches and boil in 2 quarts of Vinegar. Make the sugar into a syrup with the other 2 quarts. Use Malaga or seedless Raisins, and mustard seed washed and dried in the sun. Crush the seed slightly when dry. Throw away the seeds of the Chilis and grind (or chop) the remainder, also the garlic and Ginger. Grind or pound them with Vinegar. Boil all together for 20 minutes. Put in *the pound of Salt just before it begins to boil. Peppers must be of the meaty kind, big Red Mexicans to be found at Delleplane's (or some Spanish place in Latin Quarter). This amount makes 9 quarts.*

LARKMEAD, 1886

There is never a day in which there is not fresh fruit in the house, besides raisins and almonds and walnuts. California is the land of plenty.

A great genius with all the eccentricities of genius.

Joaquin Miller is a great genius with all the eccentricities of genius. He says he never means to work anymore. He says he has enough land to keep him from want. He has just built a house for his mother, fitted up the largest room as a tent, and is looking about for bits of color to hang the walls with. Will put up a silken banner here and there, a lady's slipper, and perhaps a pretty stocking. I suggested a petticoat for a poet's banner. He wants ribbons and satins and all manner of gay things. Says he thinks of raiding a seminary.

Joaquin told me of his embryo poem. Says I first suggested the poem to him, that I had discovered his mission - to speak for Alaska - that she lay like the sleeping beauty, voiceless and dumb, and that he was the prince to awaken her, to speak for her. He has been thinking it over and is shaping his thoughts into a great poem. Thinks he can write something "recklessly original."

I asked him to write for me the lines he wrote on the death of Peter Cooper, the great philanthropist, as I had forgotten some of them. So he wrote them with this very pen, but he writes so badly that I could not read the manuscript and I got him to read them to me and here they are. "Oh wisest is he in this whole wide land of hoarding til bent I pray. For all you can hold in your cold dead hand is what you have given away."

My dear friend Mr. Shaw arrived by morning train and walked up, there being no one to meet him at the station as he did not write. Very glad to see him and have Joaquin Miller meet him. By a singular coincidence I talked of him to Mr. Miller all the way up on the rail road Friday. After dinner, we sat a long time on the piazza enjoying the moonlight, the beautiful view and the pleasant air. Then we went in, and after Mr.

Miller had sung "Twickenham Ferry," we had a little game of cards and I won a dollar. Mr. Shaw lost 45 cents, Mr. Miller won 1 cent and Lillie lost 20 cents. We had a good deal of fun for the money.

Schram comes over tonight and tells us of the wonderful rich ore on his place and ours. Says Tichnor has assayed a ton and found 8,000 dollars in gold, besides quicksilver. Wants me to join him in building a furnace for roasting the ore, but I have no faith. Tichnor is such a fraud.

❧

Had a frightful dream. Lillie and I were in a sleeping room in which there was an immense black and white snake. It was not dead, but was tied by the neck to the wall, its coils heaped up on the floor. I was not afraid because I thought it secure and I estimated its length at three yards or nine feet. It was not a poisonous snake. Lillie and I discussed it. I was in bed and fell asleep and she told me that two other black snakes, two feet long, came into the room while I slept. When I rose to attack them, they were gone, but scorpions and toads and other reptiles came in our corner of the room. After a while, I missed the great chained serpent and found that he had escaped. Was much worried, and Lillie told me Mase had turned it loose and that it had gone back to Schram's. Woke up in great trouble, as snakes in dreams are unlucky and forebode enemies. If I could have killed them, it would have been lucky. I daresay the roast pork I ate at dinner gave birth to them.

Intended to have gone to Lonely, but Mr. Shaw and Mr. Miller came into the breakfast room while I was taking my cup of tea and were so charming that I could not tear myself away. Mr. Shaw told me much of his book. Thinks he will be able to publish it next year. If he writes as well as he talks, it will be simply irresistible.

Made more plum pickles today. More than 35 lbs. in all. Put the corn in the sun to dry. Walked thro' the vegetable garden - quantities of okra, tomatoes, potatoes, beans, squashes, salsify, cauliflower, cabbages, peas, turnips, parsnips, carrots, beets, celery, radishes, onions, lettuce, corn, leeks, horseradish and melons. The artichokes are getting too old, but new ones are coming.

Walked thro' the vegetable garden.

California is the land of plenty.

Got a telegraphic drawing of Louisiana lottery and my tickets drew nothing. I deserve disappointment for not profiting by my long experience. My bad luck extends to poor Eugenie who will be most affected by it, for she sets her heart upon winning. Lillie had several tickets but drew nothing - except a long breath.

Soon went on the early train to St. Helena and brought back a tall Heathen to take his place. Lillie paid Soon. He says he is going to Wichita, Kansas to work with Hugh who wrote him. He expects to make money as a bookkeeper.

Found Lillie in the kitchen teaching the new cook to stuff the turkey. I dressed it with fringed paper and pink ribbons and rosebuds.

To Roast a Turkey

Clean and wash the bird. Make a stuffing with one pound sausage meat, 1 cup bread crumbs, tablespoon of boiled onion cut fine, black pepper and salt to taste, tablespoon butter, 1 egg beaten well, half a can chopped truffles. Cover the turkey with pork (salt fat) cut thin, tie it on, then tie up the turkey in a sheet of well buttered letter paper. Bake for three quarters of an hour. Then take off the paper and finish baking, basting every five minutes until done.

Lillie has sent away one cook and has got another, but does not know if he will suit. People who live in the country have many vexations.

By the gate at Larkmead grew tall red hollyhocks.

The Birthday Barbeque

Mrs. Coit's birthday came late in August, and it was a regular custom to have a barbecue. Songs were specially written for this frolic and a ceremonial dance done around the roasting pig. By the gate at Larkmead grew tall red hollyhocks. Returning from a drive one day, Joaquin Miller exclaimed, "Look! The flaming sword that guards the gates of Paradise." Every guest entered that gate happily and left reluctantly.

FLORIDE GREEN

For Lillie's birthday, Floride sent Lillie a box for cards covered with chamois and ornamented with paintings of packs of cards, the four aces on the top, and red, white and green checks on the sides. Someone else sent a case of cologne water.

Made two freezers of peach ice cream, packed china, glass, silver, nine bottles of wine, two gallon pitchers of claret punch, 6 large watermelons, 8 loaves of bread, butter, sugar, limes, grapes, peaches, nectarines, apples. Lillie went up early with Buster to fish, caught a dozen speckled trout and we carried 6 large ones from the ponds, also quantities of sweet corn. The Lymans and Mrs. Noland, Mrs. Hooker and husband, Dr. and Mrs. Whitney, Mr. Chenery and Lt. Stevens of the Navy, Eugene Dewey, Joe Clarke, Maggie Randolph, the Misses Bourne, in all, seventeen persons besides the servants. Andrew had the pig over the pit and we all took turns basting it for luck. The spot was a lovely one by the creek, large and clear, surrounded by a thick forest of redwoods, the ground strewn with ferns and rustic seats. All danced and sang the song written for the occasion by Lt. Stevens. Very, very jolly.

◈

Arose early, went to Larkmead where I found Lillie and Mrs. Whitney still in their beds. Mrs. Whitney was rouged and powdered and looked like an actress on the wane. She is as artificial in character as in appearance, but is bright and witty and considered pretty.

The spot was a lovely one.

Today is my darling Lillie's birthday and I feel as if I could never give thanks enough for her preservation through so many years full of so many chances and changes, so many perils by land and by water, so many sorrows and vicissitudes. I pray my Heavenly Father always to keep her from evil and danger, to purify and chasten her with His holy spirit and finally, to bring her to life everlasting.

≈

Arose at six in the morning, Lillie and Ned Hall were to go fishing, but they did not appear, being busy getting plates and spoons and knives and forks and wine and bread and ice and fruit and corn and sweet potatoes and cake and ice cream, of which I made eight quarts with pure cream and peaches frozen together. The peaches are chopped very fine and to a quart of them I add a quart of fine sugar and a quart pure cream. Jim and I worked very hard at it. All the supplies had to be hauled a mile up the canyon to the barbeque ground. Andrew and Tom were up at two o'clock in the morning and made the fire. The pig was put over the pit of coals and was ready at one.

Ned caught the trout, fifteen beautiful ones averaging two and a half pounds each, and Lillie caught a good many small ones. About twelve, Lillie's four-in-hand drove up with Mrs. Hagar, Mrs. and Doctor Whitney, Eugene Dewey, Henry Jerome, and Mrs. Hasworth, Mr. Unger, Captain Fletcher, Miss Harrison, Joe Grant and Ned Hall. Dr. Birdsall and Nina also arrived, then the Kinkel boys, who brought the fine buck they killed this morning, which weighed a hundred fourteen pounds, which was hung up to a tree, its beautiful head and antlers decorated with ribbons.

Lillie's Birthday. Lovely morning, all up by nine. Breakfast over, we prepare for the barbecue. Sent for ice but the train passed without leaving any, altho' Philip was there. I heard wagon wheels and then a whistle at the gate. It was Herman Schram with the ice. The Messenger had forgotten to throw it off and Herman, luckily being in town to hear public speaking, brought it to me.

Jim and I pack all the plates, knives, forks, spoons, napkins, provisions. Send up ice chest with 50 lbs. ice, 1 dozen bottles beer, wine, brandy, a demijohn of whiskey which Eugene brought as a present, the pig, ham of venison, bread, sack of green corn, basket of peaches, nectarines, grapes. Prepare peaches and cream for Jim to freeze. It takes a long time, and I tire of waiting. Mrs. Vandwater and Sallie Thibauld arrive, leave their phaeton and go up in our wagon. The Smiths drive by with their four-in-hand, 2 fat Irish nurses and a wagon full of children. I did not invite them.

The barbeque was delicious, the corn not quite so good, the venison good, and the ice cream delicious. Spent the time pleasantly under the trees beside the brook enjoying quantities of lemonade and champagne cup.

Champagne Cup (#1)	Champagne Cup (#2)
1 bottle of Champagne	1 Bottle Champagne
2 bottles of Soda Water	3 wine glasses Sherry
1 sprig flowering Borage	1 glass Curacao
2 or 3 slices of Cucumber	4 slices Lemon
1 glass Brandy	2 slices Cucumber
1 lb of Ice	1 bottle Soda Water
2 ounces Powdered Sugar	1/2 lb Ice

Calistoga

The Geysers

Mr. Foss stood six feet two inches in his stockings, weighed two hundred and thirty pounds, was strong as a giant, and had the voice of a tragedian. A man of great nerve, you could not yoke up six of the most vicious of the mustang tribe that he would not tone them down shortly. Called the "King of Drivers," he would whirl around curves on high grade road at a gait that would stiffen the hair on the head of a timid tourist.

INDEPENDENT CALISTOGIAN, 1885

Lillie goes to the Geysers with a large party today. Mr. and Mrs. LeBreton, Maggie Randolph, Bob Hastings and Eugene Dewey. Eugene invited them and was host and all were loud in praise of his generosity and thoughtfulness. They go from Larkmead to Calistoga in Lillie's wagon, and from there, Foss takes them in a special stage to the Geysers where they spend some hours and return by moonlight. A very dangerous and tiresome journey which they call pleasure!

Fossville

The trip to the Geysers has always been one of the most pleasant reminiscences of the California tourist or pleasure seeker, combining as it does a ride over what is probably the finest mountain road in the State with a visit to one of nature's laboratories. One fine day, not long since, we were taken in charge by Col. Foss to be delivered at the Geysers.

Leaving Calistoga about 11:30 am, at twelve o'clock we arrived at Fossville, the residence of the Colonel. Here we found a most tempting luncheon awaiting us, prepared under the personal supervision of Mrs. Foss. After lunch we were summoned to take our place in the stage and started at a rapid rate on the twenty mile drive to the Geysers. The road passes through Knight's Valley for several miles and although extremely dusty, a light wind bears the dust away.

Finally, we enter the hills. The road from this point, until we reach the summit at an elevation of 3,500 feet and 15 miles distant, is a continual ascent. Up higher and higher stretches the road, following the windings of the hills and mountains, and in places driving the traveler almost wild with the multiplicity of its curves. On the right of us Mt. St. Helena, scarred and weather beaten, towers majestically aloft. As we dash along, quail, rabbits, squirrels, and occasionally, a deer, are startled from their hiding places and hurriedly seek quieter retreats in the hills. At length, rounding a curve in the road, a most enchanting view presents itself and Foss obligingly reigns in his horses to allow his passengers to get the full beauty of the panorama spread at their feet.

A most enchanting view

Many feet below, the hills are scattered around in reckless profusion, as if during a terrible storm at sea the waves were to be suddenly solidified. Beyond, the grainfields of Knight's Valley dotted with majestic oaks are spread out like a vast carpet. Further off, Sonoma Valley extends many miles to the bay of San Francisco, and far in the distance Mt. Tamalpais, on the northern side of the Golden Gate, shows up plainly 80 miles away.

Looking down the canyon below, we can trace for miles the three mineral-bearing ledges, parallel to each other, about a quarter of a mile apart. These ledges are the continuation of those to the northeast of Pine Flat where so much money was expended some years ago when the excitement over the discovery of

Rounding curve after curve.

quicksilver was at its height. Prospect holes, mine shafts, tunnels, dumps and cabins mark the places where men labored day after day in search of wealth.

On we go again, and higher still we ascend until we reach the little village of Pine Flat, now almost deserted. Built up in a day almost, it ran its brief, feverish existence and its prosperity is now but a tale of the past. It is estimated that over a million and a half of dollars were spent in prospecting in the district about Pine Flat.

We change horses here and with a fresh team we are swept rapidly up the mountains. Now, the trees have nearly all disappeared and naught is to be seen above us but the low, scrubby chimesal. Rounding curve after curve, we emerge upon the side of the mountain and a magnificent view of the Sonoma and Russian River Valleys is spread before us. In the distance, toward the setting sun, a well defined streak of dark blue proclaims the presence of the Pacific Ocean.

We commence our descent. From here it is a distance of five miles to the Geysers, a descent of over 1,800 feet. You can go down in a very short time, but it takes an hour and a half to get up again. The road winds in and out, there being no less than 35 curves between the summit and the Geysers. We look down into a deep canyon, the side of which is so steep that we cannot see the foot of the cliff. At the bottom is a rocky creek bed with, here and there, a quiet pool such as anglers love.

Something is loose somewhere.

About a mile and a half down we pass the Little Geysers where, in the early morning and on cold days, jets of steam rise from the earth in many places. Almost the entire distance from here into the Geysers, the road is shaded by tall stately trees, in our opinion the most delightful portion of the drive. At 5 o'clock we pull up at the Geyser Hotel, W. Forsythe, proprietor.

The Geysers are located in two small canyons which enter the main canyon directly across from the hotel. As soon as one enters the small canyon he realizes that something is loose somewhere. Sulphurous odors assail you on every hand. Clouds of steam rush from fissures in the ground with a deafening roar. The solid earth shakes beneath the feet. The canyon is full of springs, hot and cold, of every hue from inky black to

Witches' Cauldron

pure limpid water, the hottest and coldest being separated only by a few inches of rock.

The trip through is rather trying to weak nerves at first, but with a careful guide it is made in safety and the "Witches' Cauldron" and "Devil's Teapot" are visited. A warm bath taken at the bath-house on Pluton Creek, and the traveler returns to the hotel with his curiosity well satisfied.

A quarter of a mile from the Geysers is the "station" of Col. Foss. Here he has built a barn, sheds, and a very nice house. The house is his especial pet, quite large and well built. On the ground floor are four rooms; a large sitting-room, a dining room and two bedrooms, all nicely furnished. The walls of the rooms are of redwood, oiled and varnished, and a look into them on a hot day cools one off at once. Climbing roses and Passion Flower vines have been planted about the house and in a few years, but little of the outside of it will be visible to the passer-by.

At one corner of the sitting room is the telephone which connects with Pine Flat, Fossville and Calistoga. Orders and messages are passing over it constantly. As

soon as the stage leaves, the number of passengers to
or from the Geysers are known and preparations can
be made to receive them.

INDEPENDENT CALISTOGIAN, 1880

St. Helena was deserted.

Wine Commissioners

*Real estate has become the sole topic of conversation on the street, and everybody talks
"boom" with such earnestness that they have come to believe it already upon us. Indeed,
the indications are not all talk, but townspeople are buying choice lots and cheap residence
properties ahead of the advancing boom.*

ST. HELENA STAR, 1887

This afternoon, two men came here to bond Larkmead for $65,000, promising Lillie
one-half of all that it sold for beyond that sum. Of course, Lillie would not consent to
any such arrangement. They presented themselves as representative of a Syndicate of
which Alex Badlam was a member, and said they were sent by him. They have landed
a good many ranches in the upper part of this valley and are trying to start a boom in
imitation of Oakland and San Jose. They have landed Thompson's ranch for
$100,000, but they did not get Larkmead!

The Shamps also refused to bond. Tom Shamp drove up just as we were sitting down to dinner and after much persuasion, he dined with us. We all laughed over the boom and the agents who wish to bond the Napa Valley. It is rumored that they have bonded seven thousand acres.

❧

A carriage passed me by the creek, and a gentleman waved to me whom I did not recognize. When I arrived at Larkmead, the carriage was waiting at the gate and two gentlemen, McLoomis and Beard, in the hall with Lillie. They are commissioners, appointed to visit the grape growing country and report on it. We prevail on them to stay all night and spend a delightful evening. We have music, and McLoomis sings delightfully. Mr. Beard tells us that McLoomis, having made himself the champion runner at Harvard College, went to England and ran against their best men and beat them. Then he came to California and married the heiress of two million dollars. He is a man of strong individuality. It was after two o'clock when we went to bed.

❧

Philip drives me to the station, where we wait more than an hour for the train. We chat with a local gentleman who takes a gloomy view of the grape business. He thinks that if the tariff is taken off foreign wines and brandies, our grapes will not be worth anything, that wine will fall to 5 cents a gallon, and all our vineyards a total loss. He thinks that there is not demand enough for the product and that everything here is overdone. He thinks people are foolish in planting so many olives as long as good oil is made from cotton seed. He has 200,000 gallons of wine in his cellar. All together, he has me quite discouraged.

Mrs. Hagar, her daughter and a friend, the latter a Miss Field from St. Louis, arrive after nine o'clock tonight. They were due here at half-past seven, but the crowd on the train was so great that they were delayed a long time. There were more than twenty car loads of Native Sons of the Golden West going to Napa City for tomorrow's celebration of the twenty-seventh anniversary of California's admission into the Union. Someone said there were a thousand eight hundred of them, all young and good looking. There will be thousands of others arriving tomorrow from different parts of the State, and there is to be a banquet and a ball and processions and speeches and horn bands and more than the usual amount of fuss and feathers.

෨

Today is Admissions Day, and these sons and daughters born in California have organized an American Party which all good citizens hope will, one day, rule the State. The ladies drove off for St. Helena, stopping at different wine cellars. Went on to Tiburcio Parrott's magnificent place "Miravalle" where we were delighted with the view and the beautiful house and its surroundings. St. Helena was deserted, as everybody had gone to Napa City to attend the reception of the Native Sons of the Golden West.

The ladies declared they enjoyed the drive. Floride Green returned with them, as she is having a holiday today and tomorrow, then resumes her work in school. She has a class of young children, a laborious life. She showed me some little cradles she had made of goose eggs with gilded rockers and little doll babies in them. She finds it difficult to get goose eggs, and I recommended she get seagull eggs, which are speckled and of many colors.

"Miravalle" where we were delighted with the view.

We sat up late playing cards and they all made fun of me. I lost a dollar, a great deal of money for a cautious woman like myself. The young ladies went to bed, but not until Emilia Hagar sang us a good many beautiful songs.

ॐ

Alex Badlam's niece and a doctor, I did not catch his name, drove here today from Calistoga to invite Miss Field to lunch with her tomorrow. I met her at the door but did not ask her in. I excused Lillie who was in bed, and also Miss Field, who I told her could not accept any invitations, not having time. I rather fancied Miss Field did not like it, but I acted for the best. If we once received Badlam's niece, she would bring all her disreputable acquaintances here at all times.

Miss Field and I sat together on the verandah and I read to her, at her request, some papers in my old journal. I was very sorry afterwards when she informed me that she meant to use it in her notes. I begged her not to and hope she will see the impropriety of doing so.

Lillie wore her Japanese kimono which is very becoming to her. Miss Field liked it so well that Lillie insisted on her trying on one of hers which had never been worn. It suited her so well that she declared her intention of investing three dollars in one as soon as she got back to town.

ॐ

Everybody slept late this morning, except the young ladies whom I managed to get off to Lonely where we gathered roses and violets and afterwards, to Schram's where they walked thro' the wine cellars, the first they had ever seen.

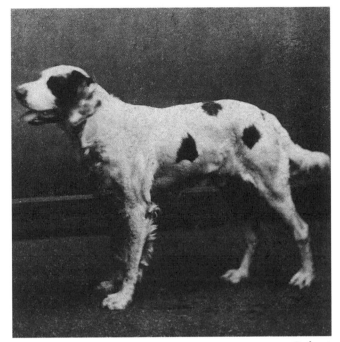

Robert

We got back to Larkmead by one o'clock and luncheoned. Mrs. Hagar, Floride Green and Lillie had been devoting themselves to photography. Mrs. Hagar took photographs of Lillie's two hound puppies, Robert and Blazer. Blazer is white with coal black ears, very long and drooping. Robert has two brown and two black spots on white ground.

&

Philip calculates the grape crop and thinks there will be 185 tons to 225 last year. 60 tons Zinfandel, 70 tons Malvoisie, 25 tons Burgers, 20 tons Reisling and 10 tons

Chasselas. Mr. Bonner sends his offer for grapes. $14 for Reislings, $13 for Zinfandels, $10 for Burgers, $7 for Malvoisie. It is a dreadful disappointment as the picking and hauling will cost more. It will not pay half Lillie's expenses of cultivation. Poor child, she looked wretchedly when she got up, after only a few hours sleep. We hurried through breakfast that our guests might get off by afternoon train.

Very cloudy and cool, and about 4 o'clock, lightning and thunder, threatening rain which I am afraid will hurt the grapes. The sky was very red in the west and the mountains all rosy. Mrs. Ambrose Bierce drove up with her little girl and delicate boy. She had been to Larkmead and not finding me, came on her way to Lonely. She told us she had found the Schrams in great trouble on account of Herman who had quarelled with his father and gone off, not to return. Of course they were in the greatest grief. Our greatest sorrows come through our affections.

૪

I saw Sam Long Sing today about employing men for grape picking, but he does not like to take a contract. Lillie saw Schram, McPike and others about the grapes. We had expected to find Mrs. Schram inconsolable, but to Lillie's surprise, Mrs. Schram was quite calm and collected and thought a year's absence and hard work would do Herman a great deal of good.

૪

Drove to Schram's to see their vineyard in its greatest perfection. Mrs. Schram and I walked from her house, climbed the steep road to the vineyard, dusty and tiresome but the view was fine and the crop of grapes immense, berries very large and clusters of many pounds weight. The vineyard is all hillside, no level land. Muscatels rich and musky, golden Chasselas, rose Chasselas, Malvoisie, Mission and Reislings, all full bunches of fruit resting upon the ground and piling themselves in pyramids around the stakes. It was a sight to enchant a grape grower.

While we were in the vineyard, the clouds overhead began to send down big drops, the thunder rolled, and the lightning flashed and Mrs. Schram and I ran for shelter under the firs at the edge of the woods where we kept dry and waited until the storm passed. Then, we made our way down a steep hill to her home and took a glass of wine. It rained steadily all afternoon, a most uncommon thing in September.

Harvest

A Most Alarming Aspect

The vintage may now be said to be at its full height and the crop will fall considerably short of last year. The yield, however, varies according to locality; in some sections we find only half a crop reported, while in others vineyardists report a great yield. There is a general complaint of too much sugar in the grapes. Winemakers fear trouble in fermentation on this account. Grape prices vary according to location and we find quite a distinction in favor of hill grapes. The poorer kinds are selling for about $10. Zinfandels from $12.50 to $14 per ton. Chasselas, Riesling and finer varieties range from $14 to as high as $17. There is a great scarcity of labor, and in many vineyards, women and children are at work. White men are paid as high as $2 a day, Chinamen $1.25, but some are demanding $1.50.

ST. HELENA STAR, 1887

There was a great commotion in the upper story at Lonely. Jim thought he had captured some animal in his trap. Sure enough, there was a beautiful mountain cat held fast by the foot. Jim made a cage and brought it to Larkmead, and we gave it grapes and sugar to eat.

*

Lillie went to St. Helena to see about getting men to pick grapes. Sam Long Sing repeats that he can only find six men and they want $1.25 a day, which is too much. She saw Schram who offered her little more for her grapes than Bonner. Also, the Uncle Sam Vineyard at Napa, but transportation is dear and troublesome. After a long waste of time, Lamonte makes his offer. $14 for Zinfandel, Chasselas and Reisling, $12 for Burgers and $10 for Malvoisie. Letter from McPike who will give $12 for Malvoisie delivered at Napa, $14 for Zinfandels and $12 for Burgers. He will buy, but not for cash.

I decide to go to St. Helena and inquire about grapes. Mase drives and we see Bonner's foreman. Bonner is in his cellar and wants an answer. I find McPike and he advises me to close with Lamonte, if he will make satisfactory payments. Pickers are very scarce and dear. I see Connor and ask him what he thinks of Lamonte, and he says Lamonte has lost heavily during the last two seasons. He advises me to sell to Bonner. I meet Lamonte on the street and he wants an answer by Sunday, as others are offering their grapes. I don't know what to do.

*

Allen Knight and wife arrived by evening train. They are so jolly and happy that they bring an atmosphere of gaiety with them and are always welcome guests. Mr. Knight told me that his wife was in a delicate condition. They have been married a long time, without any children, and I hope this event will not make them less happy.

When I came to breakfast, I had to wait half an hour, as Allen Knight was taking a photo of the dining room and wanted his instrument in place for two hours.

૩૦

It is the anniversary of Knickerbocker Number 5, and there is a banquet in San Francisco tonight at the Maison Doree. Lillie sent the flowers for their table decorations. At Larkmead, Allen Knight, Porter Garnett, Mase Kinkel, Mrs. Knight and Lillie improvised fire hats and belts and marched around the hall and sang fire songs and made merry. Mr. Knight photographed Lillie, his wife, Porter and himself in their fire hats. At dinner everyone drank to Number 5 a good many times in champagne and other wines. Porter told some stories an old fireman had told him of Lillie's early life. After, he put a new string on Lillie's banjo which consumed all his energy and made him quite limp. Music and charades until after midnight, some of the charades very good. "Conundrum," "Matrimony," "Isinglass," "Barbecue," "Metaphysician," "Phantom," and others. I went to bed late, and others not at all.

Arose just as Lillie was coming to bed. She had sat up all night. Said she had been balancing her grape account with Mase and ascertained that she will pay out more for picking and delivery than she will receive for the sale of the grapes.

૩૦

Got a fright about Porter. He was missing several hours, but was only fishing up the creek. He leaves today after a long visit. Lillie was very sorry to have him go, but his

Mr. Knight photographed Lillie, his wife, Porter and himself in their fire hats.

family wanted him to return to San Francisco to go to the Business College. He promises to come again when he has a vacation.

Lillie's guests arose late and after breakfast, lounged idly in the hall looking at photos and engravings. Mrs. Knight walked with me through the vineyard where six Chinese men are picking grapes. Then to Lonely, where we found everything so peaceful and tranquil and restful and cool and shady that we sat in armchairs on the verandah and enjoyed ourselves. On the way back to Larkmead, we met Mr. Knight, on the way with Mase to Tubbs' cellar.

Mase made an earnest appeal to Tubbs to take Lillie's Zinfandels, which are dying upon the vines. Tubbs simply said his tanks were full. There was no fermentation. He had no right to engage more grapes than he could receive, but after doing so, he ought to have bought more tanks. He has no right to refuse to receive the grapes after buying them and is liable to prosecution for the loss caused by such refusal, but no one wants a lawsuit, especially no woman.

Saw a great fire burning in the direction of Calistoga and heard that it was Robert's fruit dryer and the surrounding forests. We could see the round, red sun through the smoke which was black and edged with flame. Then, there blazed up a great fire back of Lonely in the valley between Napa and Sonoma and it raged with great violence, burning the tall firs and redwoods and doing incalculable damage. It had a most alarming aspect!

Her hunting suit was made by Poole of London.

Deer Stalking

Mrs. Coit was a splendid shot and the hall at Larkmead was filled with trophies of the chase. Her hunting suit was made by Poole of London, a white shirt with a stiff front and high collar, a jacket and a skirt which escaped the ground about ten inches, a very extreme innovation.

FLORIDE GREEN

October is golden. Oscar came down this morning from Bear Flat with a message from Lillie who was up there deer hunting with Captain Hooker and the Kinkels. They set off last evening with hounds Sounder, Echo, Roller and Belle, and the Kinkels took their pack. Lillie says some hunters got eight deer last week in the canyon. They walked all over Wind Whistle, up Teal's canyon to Bear Flat, were gone all night, and got three fine deer which delights them. Lillie wanted bacon and bread and potatoes, which I sent by Oscar.

At ten, the rest of her party, Mrs. Hooker, Eugene Dewey, Miss Ruhl and Lt. and Mrs. Chenery, drove over on their way to the picnic ground where they were to meet the hunters and have breakfast. I gave them some butter and eggs, a demijohn of cider and some bottles of wine, and promised to join them.

It was two o'clock when I arrived, and they were all having a jolly time. Mrs. Hooker and Miss Ruhl had made the omelette and coffee and fried the potatoes and the table was covered with delicacies. Stewed quails, roast beef and ham, wines and fruit. At four, I left with Eugene and Miss Ruhl, but the rest went hunting, and at eight o'clock came back with a fine buck, the happiest hunting party I ever saw.

Game Pie

Cut some thin slices of Venison, well pepper and salt them, and lay them at the bottom of a very deep dish. Cut up 2 quail, 2 pigeons, and a hare, and lay them in pieces. Add 2 mutton kidneys, a teacup full of pickled mushrooms, forcemeat balls, egg balls, and a good gravy made from the bones of the game and some stock. If served hot send up with cover on; if cold fill up with good aspic jelly.

At breakfast, Captain Hooker showed me the clever sketches he had made of the picnic and deer hunt. He and Lt. Chenery sang the new song he has just written, "The Larkmead Squad." They are both very clever men.

Lillie took me to see the venison, and I advised her how to distribute it. A haunch to Mrs. Hooker, a "back strap" to Eugene, Lt. Chenery a forequarter, and one for me. The head is to be stuffed for Lillie.

Hunting party

Examined he wine which Philip muddled with. Test with saccharometer and find the fermentation is not yet complete. Drove to Mrs. Schram with a bottle and asked for her advice. I looked at her new cellar and saw Schram with a railroad agent.

Floride and I went to the library and returned with four volumes. Floride wishes to copy birds and fishes and beasts and insects to paint on cards for the Christmas holidays. She is very industrious.

Prepared quinces for preserving and made jelly. It rained at intervals and Tong came from Larkmead and put the corn in the loft. After dinner, it cleared off and the stars shone and large horned owls were hooting in the trees near the house.

ॐ

The coldest morning I have felt this winter altho' the little boy is out, indicating a change. The two little Tucker girls walked up to inquire after me. They are both pretty, the youngest a beauty with very black eyes and curly golden hair. I gave them cakes and raisins.

At Larkmead, Eugenie made a fire in the dining room and we had lunch. She brought me salmon and all the papers. Afterwards, Lillie drove with Eugenie to see the young Jersey bull she has given Bob Hastings for a wedding present. He is to be sent from Calistoga tomorrow by freight train.

Saw in the papers the dreadful tragedy in the Bierce family. My heart ached for the stricken parents, the beautiful mother, the gifted father, prostrated by this dreadful blow. Their eldest son, Raymond Bierce, was to have been married last Sunday evening to a girl of seventeen. That afternoon, she eloped with Raymond's best friend and best man and married him in Sacramento. This morning, Raymond shot him, wounding him fatally. Then he shot the girl, put the pistol to his own head, and fell dead.

Chinatown

Ritchie Creek

Mase and Chinese men are unloading pine poles at the creek bank where I shall build pens to stop the overflow. I counted nearly 60 trunks of what had been beautiful fir trees and it caused me a pang.

> One happy result has already followed the anti-Chinese movement in St. Helena. The ground on which our present Chinatown now stands has been purchased by a committee from the anti-Coolie League. The trade was quietly negotiated with Mr. Gillam last week by Judge Elgin, who secured a contract on the premises for $1,600. The deed has been placed on record and the undesirable tenants given due notice to quit the premises. It is said that Mr. Gillam, after signing the contract, had offers of much larger sums from representatives of six Chinese companies, but the above is a happy and peaceable solution of one phase of the Chinese problem. The land, we understand, will be rented to a firm for the establishment of a lumber yard and sash and door factory.
>
> ST. HELENA STAR, 1886

Drove to Burgess to see him about the creek. He wants me to send two men for a day or two to deepen the creek channel. Burgess told me all arrangements for a station at Larkmead had been made. Tucker was to give the water and sell an acre of his land for 125 dollars which was to be paid for by Schram and that Bale Station was to be abolished and the switch removed to Larkmead which will, in fact, be bad for us. All that beastly old Schram's work! This is my birthday and I must keep my temper. I am 63 years old today. It is the anniversary of my darling's marriage and she always keeps it as a fast.

Porter came with me to the Palace Hotel.

Larkmead Christmas

Our reporter took a stroll around town Friday morning to see which stores had made a specialty of carrying Christmas goods and he was astonished at the large number in which he had found Holiday displays. There are persons in this town, as in all others, who have an idea that they can do much better in purchasing presents by going to San Francisco. To all such, the Star would whisper "it's a mistake."

ST. HELENA STAR, 1884

Leave for San Francisco on the four o'clock train. At Vallejo there was a heavy fog, and I waited three quarters of an hour for the ferry. Altogether, an hour and a half behind time when Porter met me at the wharf and came with me to the Palace Hotel where I found Lillie with Mr. and Mrs. Hooker. Mr. Hooker went out and got me some nice roasted oysters in a loaf of bread.

Market and Jones Streets

Went to breakfast at Swan's and afterwards wandered about, looking in the shop windows at the holiday presents. Bought half a dozen handkerchiefs for Mase, a pair of gauntlets for Tong and a pair for Jim and a cravat and matchbox for Philip. Lillie got a match box for Jim and a pipe for Philip. Went to the East Indian shop and got a fan of peacock feathers for Lillie. Then to Ichi Ban, the new Japanese store, and saw many odd things.

Lillie received a box of cut flowers and Eugene sent me a large basket of magnificent flowers, scarlet velvety Poinsettias and azeleas and roses and violets and maidenhair ferns and carnations and hyacinths and begonias and everything sweet and lovely.

The Palace Hotel

Carey Friedlander called with a large bunch of violets for Lillie and told us about the amateur theatrical performance at the Tevis'. It was fairly done, a very sensible way of amusing idle fashionable people. We called at the Lick House for the Whitneys and went to the Poodle Dog. The table was ready but the cook was drunk and nothing was as good as usual, except the terrapin.

≥∘

Went shopping today, or rather wandered around looking at the Christmas things on exhibition. At twelve I went to Lillie's cooking class, where were Mrs. Hooker, Mrs. Fox and Lillie, all busy at their lesson. Afterwards, a good luncheon for fifty cents. Walked up California street to Kearney, where I met the author of *Years in California*. He

"Me gawd, I've left all me money at home!"

Porter Garnett

offered to send me his book, but I told him I had already read it. Then he proposed that I should give him a portion of my journal to be incorporated in his new edition. I told him that would be impossible.

The town is excited over the expected arrival of the Globe Galloper Nellie Bly, who is expected to arrive any moment on the China steamer. The press will meet her with a tug and carry her to a special train waiting for her at Oakland, so as to lose no time. She will go by Atlantic & Pacific Railroad, the Central Pacific stopped by snow. There are several trains and hundreds of passengers snowbound in the Sierra. My sympathies are with the Southern girl who is steaming across the Atlantic on a slow steamer, but luck is against the South.

Henry came and I sent him to buy lottery tickets for Philip (five) and one which I will give to Eugenie for Christmas. It is No. 37313, all odd numbers. Philip's five numbers are 22663, 62479, 42284, 57514, 15624. Henry paid the money (six dollars) and I am to pay him.

෨

Mrs. Honolulu Hastings and Porter Garnett were with us and we had champagne frappe and a large pound cake and sat up 'til three o'clock. Porter showed us all his magic lantern. Mrs. Hastings told us of the wild peacocks which used to oversee their estate on one of the Sandwich Islands and of the guards they kept around their garden to prevent the peacocks from devouring it. Then she told us of her experiences in London with Queen Kapiolani when she went to Queen Victoria's jubilee. She and her husband will sail Christmas Day for Honolulu and I feel very sorry, for somehow she strikes my fancy.

And the champagne poured like water.

Joaquin Miller called at the Palace Hotel looking well and happy. He brought with him his new volume, which he has dedicated to "Dear Lil' H. Coit, the dearest and best of Californians - as we were boys together and you have been true blue all these long years, without your permission, I have dedicated this book to you. Read it, the dedication I mean, then deliver the book to the Bohemians. Xmas, 1888. Yours, Joaquin Miller."

He seems very much enamored of his mountain ranch. We are all so in the beginning, but when we have exhausted our enthusiasm and our energies and our means, without any benefit therefrom, we are not so much in love with ranches as we were. Mr. Miller was in high spirits, telling about his fruit tree planting which runs into the thousands. Two hundred apple trees from Nova Scotia. I did not know before that apple trees grew in Nova Scotia. Two hundred peach trees from New Jersey. Two hundred Carolina poplars, I presume he means the tulip tree. He told me that he worked out of doors on rainy days, changing his clothes twice a day. He also told me about his fish ponds, his goldfish, carp and trout. I envy him the pleasure of planting and watching the growth of things. There is no pleasure like it. I know what it is to make an Eden out of a wilderness.

≈

Six members of Lillie's old Knickerbocker fire brigade called and presented her with a handsome silver Christmas card, very large and massive in a fine blue velvet case. The card was engraved, "A Merry Christmas to Mrs. Lillie Hitchcock Coit from Knickerbocker Association No. 5." They made her a little speech to which she responded by saying, "let's take a drink," and the champagne poured like water.

It is a short journey to the ranch.

It is a short journey to the ranch but a very tiresome one on account of the many changes. In the first place, I have to take the street car to the wharf, then I take the ferry boat to Oakland Mole, then the train for Vallejo Junction, then the steamer cross the Straights of Carquinez, then the train to Bale Station, then a carriage to Lonely.

⁂

Christmas Day! It dawned pleasantly upon us all. Cook made a garland of evergreens and Christmas berries for the dining room at Larkmead, and Eugenie made wreaths and hung them. All of us got presents. I got a pair of knitted slippers from Floride and a letter from Mallie Garnett, at school in Exeter. He goes to Harvard next year. A promising youth, I am very fond of him.

Lillie got a gorgeous table scarf from her namesake in Arizona - of green silk covered with tiger lilies and fringed with strips from buckskin a la Apache Indian. Also, a knitted wrap for the shoulders from Floride with some nice handpainted Christmas cards. Lillie gave a box of fine embroidered handkerchiefs to Floride.

I gave Mase a shaving case with razor, Cook his watch and Eugenie $5. Lillie gave Cook a pair of gloves and Mase a good silver watch. She gave Eugenie $20. To me, she gave a journal and a wastebasket which I wanted, and a beautiful black onyx brooch in a shape like a pansy with a fine diamond in the center.

We had a splendid dinner. Oysters and salmon trout and an entree of foie gras and the great turkey which was perfectly cooked with cranberries and celery and sweet potatoes, and three squash pies which Lillie made herself, and a great plum pudding blazing blue with brandy, all of which went to the servants, who had a good dinner in the kitchen with all the wine they could drink.

Larkmead

Epilogue

Mase met me at the station, and we drove to Larkmead which looked ill-cultivated, grassy and ragged. The rose bushes and grapevines were unkempt and over grown. Grass was growing in the walls, the doors and windows boarded up.

Mase and I put the storeroom in order. The floor was covered several inches deep with almond shells and the sacks were all empty. A large rat which was hidden among the boxes rushed out. It took us a long time to move the bottles and jars and glasses and china and preserves, pickles, canned fruit and meats.

One might stand a siege with such a supply.

Appendix 1: Sources used in compiling the text

THE HITCHCOCK DIARIES are part of the Hitchcock Coit Papers, Special Collections, F. W. Olin Library, Mills College. These Papers include twenty-three volumes of diaries (1872-97) by Martha Hitchcock, as well as letters, photographs, newsclippings, and all manner of ephemera relating to the Hitchcock family. To create an accessible text, diary excerpts from 1875 through 1895 have been edited and arranged by the authors according to the seasons of a year. The narrative seeks to capture the gesture and odd detail, evocative of a particular world of grace and style. Selection and recasting is neither scholarly nor literal. For this reason, the text is presented in a prose format, without apparatus such as ellipses or annotations. Spelling and punctuation have been standardized where necessary.

MH Diary refers to the manuscript diaries of Martha Hitchcock in the Hitchcock Coit Papers, Special Collections Department, F. W. Olin Library, Mills College. The year designates the volume. The citation for the diaries is always listed first; citations for other material are listed as they appear in the text.

Introduction:

"Napa Valley...," *St. Helena Star*, 1888.

Chapter 1 Roses in Winter:

MH Diary, 1879; 1884; 1885; 1887; 1888; 1889; 1890.

"A crowd gathered...," *Independent Calistogian*, 1889.

"Chicken Fricassee," Lillie Hitchcock Coit, Recipe Book, ca. 1870-80 (BANC MSS 95/24 c), The Bancroft Library, University of California, Berkeley.

"The heaviest rain...," *St. Helena Star*, 1884.

Chapter 2 Soon the Chinese Cook and a Fat French Maid:

MH Diary, 1879; 1881; 1882; 1883; 1885; 1886.

Green, Floride, *Some Personal Recollections of Lillie Hitchcock Coit*-5 (San Francisco: Grabhorn Press, 1935), 30.

Garnett, Porter, "An Equivocal Equine Excerpt," Hitchcock Coit Papers, F.W. Olin Library, Mills College.

"Sweet Pickle," Lillie Hitchcock Coit, Recipe Book, ca. 1870–80 (BANC MSS 94–5/24 c), The Bancroft Library, University of California, Berkeley.

"Among the numerous grape-growers ...," *Independent Calistogian*, 1889.

Chapter 3 Miss Hastings' Engagement Visit:

MH Diary, 1879; 1881; 1882; 1889; 1890; 1893; 1895.

"To show how well...," *St. Helena Star*, 1888.

Chapter 4 A Midsummernight Astronomy Lecture:

MH Diary, 1881; 1885; 1887.

Green, Floride, 32-3.

"Pound Cake," Lillie Hitchcock Coit, Recipe Book, ca. 1870–80 (BANC MSS 94–5/24 c), The Bancroft Library, University of California, Berkeley.

Chapter 5 Ain't We Jolly?:

This chapter is comprised of excerpts from the *St. Helena Star*, 1884 and 1888, and the *Independent Calistogian*, 1888.

Chapter 6 God's White Tomatoes:

MH Diary, 1875; 1881; 1886; 1887; 1889; 1890; 1893.

Green, Floride, 33-4.

"Green Tomato Pickle," Lillie Hitchcock Coit, Recipe Book, ca. 1870-80 (BANC MSS 95/24 c), The Bancroft Library, University of California, Berkeley.

"Peach Chutney," Lillie Hitchcock Coit, Recipe Book, ca. 1870-80 (BANC MSS 95/24 c), The Bancroft Library, University of California, Berkeley.

"To Roast a Turkey," Lillie Hitchcock Coit, Recipe Book, ca. 1870-80 (BANC MSS 95/24 c), The Bancroft Library, University of California, Berkeley.

Chapter 7 The Birthday Barbecue:

MH Diary, 1881; 1887.

Green, Floride, 29.

"Champagne Cups," Lillie Hitchcock Coit, Recipe Book, ca. 1870-80 (BANC MSS 95/24 c), The Bancroft Library, University of California, Berkeley.

Chapter 8 The Geysers:

MH Diary, 1881; 1882.

"Mr. Foss stood...," *Independent Calistogian,* 1885.

"The trip to the Geysers...," *Independent Calistogian,* 1880.

Chapter 9 Wine Commissioners:

MH Diary, 1882; 1887; 1888.

"Real estate...," *St. Helena Star,* 1887.

Chapter 10 A Most Alarming Aspect:

MH Diary, 1881; 1887; 1890.

"The vintage...," *St. Helena Star,* 1887.

Chapter 11 Deer Stalking:

MH Diary, 1881; 1887; 1889; 1895.

Green, Floride, 30.

"Game Pie," Lillie Hitchcock Coit, Recipe Book, ca. 1870-80 (BANC MSS 95/24 c), The Bancroft Library, University of California, Berkeley.

"One happy result...," *St. Helena Star,* 1886.

Chapter 12 Larkmead Christmas:

MH Diary, 1881; 1882; 1886; 1887; 1889; 1890; 1895.

"Our reporter...," *St. Helena Star*, 1884.

Epilogue:

MH Diary, 1881.

Appendix 2: Photographs

All photographs are from the late nineteenth century. Additional information is provided where available. Where not otherwise credited, items are from the Hitchcock Coit Papers, F.W. Olin Library, Mills College.

Introduction:

Man in garden. p. 6.

Martha & Lillie Hitchcock. Daguerreotype. p. 12.

Howard Coit. p. 15

Lillie Hitchcock Coit. p. 15

MAP. O.H. Buckman, Napa County, California, [1895]. Scale 1:51,000. Detail. Reproduced from an original in the collections of the Geography and Map Division, Library of Congress. p. 16-17.

Martha Hitchcock. p. 20.

Chapter 1 Roses in Winter:

Calistoga Depot, east corner (Northeast from Calistoga Hotel). Photograph by Turrill and Miller. Courtesy, The Society of California Pioneers. p. 22.

Larkmead. pp. 26-7.

St. Helena downtown. Courtesy, Sharpsteen Museum, Calistoga. pp. 32-3.

Chapter 2 Soon the Chinese Cook and a Fat French Maid:

Ah Hing. Courtesy, Napa Valley Museum. p. 34.

Porter Garnett. Courtesy, The Bancroft Library. p. 36.

Schram family. Courtesy, Sharpsteen Museum, Calistoga. p. 40.

Chinese men, Napa Valley. Private collection. p. 42.

The house at Lonely. p. 44.

Lillie Hitchcock Coit. p. 45.

Chapter 3 Miss Hastings' Engagement Visit:

Guests at Larkmead with Lillie Hitchcock Coit in foreground. p. 48.

Picnic party, Napa Valley. Courtesy, Sharpsteen Museum, Calistoga. pp. 52-3.

Martha Hitchcock, Lonely. p. 55.

Chapter 4 A Midsummernight Astronomy Lecture:

Guests on lawn, Larkmead. p. 58.

Hicklin Cherry Orchard. Courtesy, The Society of California Pioneers. pp. 62-3.

Professor and Mrs. John LeConte. Courtesy, The Bancroft Library. p. 65.

White Sulphur Springs, ca. 1860. Courtesy, Seward and Betty Foote, White Sulphur Springs Retreat and Spa. p. 66.

Chapter 5 Ain't We Jolly?:

Forni family, Napa Valley, Fourth of July, 1883. Courtesy, Napa Valley Museum. p. 68.

Native Sons of the Golden West, Calistoga. Courtesy, Sharpsteen Museum, Calistoga. pp. 72-3.

Refreshment wagon, St. Helena Bottling and Cold Drink Co., 1883. Postcard, ca. 1910. Courtesy, Napa Valley Museum. p. 75.

Chapter 6 God's White Tomatoes:

Joaquin Miller, April 20, 1896. Photograph by Floride Green, inscribed by Joaquin Miller, "For Mrs. Lillie Coit." p. 76.

Joaquin Miller. Courtesy, The Bancroft Library. p. 80.

Ambrose's Garden. p. 83.

Orange Trees, Dunaweal. Courtesy, The Society of California Pioneers. pp. 84-5.

Ambrose Valerio, Lonely. p. 86.

Chapter 7 The Birthday Barbecue:

Man reclining on lawn, Larkmead. p. 88.

Redwood trees ("Dunaweal," near Calistoga). Photograph by Turill and Miller. Courtesy, The Society of California Pioneers. p. 91.

Chapter 8 The Geysers:

Calistoga. Stereoscopic photograph by Eadweard Muybridge. Courtesy, The Bancroft Library. p. 94.

Geyser Springs stage coach at Fossville. Stereoscopic photograph by Andrew Price. Courtesy, Sharpsteen Museum, Calistoga. p. 96.

Geyser Springs stage coach en route to Geyser Springs. Stereoscopic photograph by Andrew Price. Courtesy, Sharpsteen Museum, Calistoga. p. 97.

Geyser Springs stage coach en route to Geyser Springs. Stereoscopic photograph by Andrew Price. Courtesy, Sharpsteen Museum, Calistoga. p. 98.

Geyser Springs stage coach at Geyser Springs. Stereoscopic photograph by Andrew Price. Courtesy, Sharpstccn Muscum, Calistoga. p. 99.

Witches' Cauldron. Stereoscopic photograph by Eadweard Muybridge. Courtesy, The Bancroft Library. p. 100.

Chapter 9 Wine Commissioners:

Main Street, St. Helena, 1886. Courtesy, Sharpsteen Museum, Calistoga. p. 102.

Hillside Olive Orchards. Courtesy, The Society of California Pioneers. pp. 106-7

Robert (dog). Photograph by Bradley and Rulofson, San Francisco. p. 109.

Chapter 10 A Most Alarming Aspect:

Vineyard, near Calistoga. Photograph by Turrill and Miller. Courtesy, The Society of California Pioneers. p. 112.

Porter Garnett, Lillie Hitchcock Coit, Allen Knight, Mrs. Knight. Photograph by Allen Knight. Courtesy, The Bancroft Library. p. 116.

Chapter 11 Deer Stalking:

Lillie Hitchcock Coit in hunting suit. Reprinted from Floride Green, *Some Personal Recollections of Lillie Hitchcock Coit*-5 (San Francisco, Grabhorn Press, 1935). p. 118.

Gentlemen and hunting dogs. p. 121.

St. Helena Chinatown, 1890. Courtesy, Sharpsteen Museum, Calistoga. p. 123.

Ritchie Creek, Lonely. p. 124.

Chapter 12 Larkmead Christmas:

Grand Court, Palace Hotel, San Francisco. Courtesy, The Bancroft Library. p. 126.

Market Street & Jones Street, San Francisco. San Francisco History Center, San Francisco Public Library. p. 128.

Palace Hotel, San Francisco. San Francisco History Center, San Francisco Public Library. p. 129.

Porter Garnett. Inscribed by Porter Garnett, "Me gord..." Courtesy, The Bancroft Library. p. 130.

Lillie Hitchcock Coit, 1898. Photograph by Taber, San Francisco. p. 132.

Passengers debarking ferry, Vallejo. Photograph by Chamberlain. Courtesy, Napa Valley Museum. p. 134.

Epilogue:

Larkmead. p. 136.